The Queen & Prince Philip

The Platinum Wedding Anniversary

The Queen & Prince Philip

The Platinum Wedding Anniversary

1947–2017

Introduction

IN AN AGE of instant gratification, high-speed communications and quick fixes, it seems almost incongruous to reflect on a relationship whose origins date back to the years of austerity and uncertainty that followed in the wake of the Second World War. Yet it is this very enduring quality, this permanence that makes the 70th anniversary of the marriage of Her Majesty The Queen and The Duke of Edinburgh so very special.

For some, their wedding day is the stuff of treasured memory; for many others, the Royal couple have been an institution as ever-present and steadfast as that of the Monarchy itself. However, The Queen and The Duke are more than mere embodiments of royalty, more, even, than a sovereign and her consort. They are much-loved individuals who have grown, led, struggled, overcome and excelled before our eyes, and who are held in the very highest regard by millions the world over.

Their joint journey – as Queen and consort, as husband and wife, and as parents, grandparents and great-grandparents – is well documented. It is in photography, however, as much as in word that the wider world is granted a window into their marriage, their relationships and their inner lives.

By bringing together some of the most exceptional photography of the Royal couple from the past 70 years, this book aims to capture something of that journey – both in and out of the public spotlight – and to join the nation, the Commonwealth and a world of admirers in wishing The Queen and The Duke of Edinburgh congratulations on the occasion of their platinum wedding anniversary.

Contents

The young Elizabeth

A *blessed* *beginning*

Born into a world of intense public interest, Princess Elizabeth's childhood was, none the less, a remarkably "normal" affair, albeit one that would eventually give way to greatness and great responsibility

THERE IS NOTHING unusual in the story of a 91-year-old who was born in a house that later gave way to an office block, who performed in pantomimes as a teenager, who trained as a car mechanic and who used ration coupons to pay for a wedding outfit. Except this is no ordinary nonagenarian, which explains why the then Home Secretary rushed to 17 Bruton Street, Mayfair in the middle of the night to attend her birth.

Sir William Joynson-Hicks certainly had other pressing concerns at the time, as a wage-related standoff with coal miners would lead to Britain's first ever general strike within a fortnight. However, tradition dictated that the Home Secretary should witness all royal births, and that of Elizabeth Alexandra Mary, daughter of The Duke and Duchess of York, who was born at the home of her maternal grandparents at 2.40 am on 21 April 1926, was no exception.

The age-old custom of verifying each royal birth in this way is said to have started when rumours were spread in 1688 that a baby passed off as King James II's son had been smuggled into the bedchamber in a warming pan because there had been no actual pregnancy. Understandably, Princess Elizabeth's paternal grandmother, Queen Mary, was less than thrilled about the Court Circular announcing that Sir William "was present in the house at the time of the birth", writing in a letter: "We did not approve of that stupid announcement, all on account of the 'confounded' etiquette. We tried to stop it but it was too late."

Since the duke's older brother, The Prince of Wales, was the heir apparent, Princess Elizabeth didn't have the pressure of being a future monarch. Nevertheless, the public took a huge interest in the royal baby, who was third in line to the throne, with crowds gathering outside the Bruton Street address even six weeks after her birth.

For her christening at Buckingham Palace at the end of May 1926, the princess wore a white satin robe that had been made for the baptism of Queen Victoria's eldest daughter in 1841. But her mother generally insisted on

Previous pages: Princess Elizabeth (left) and younger sister Margaret in a carriage in the grounds of the Royal Lodge in Windsor, 1940

Opposite: The Duke and Duchess of York (later King George VI and Queen Elizabeth, The Queen Mother) with their daughter Elizabeth, in 1926

"I don't think any child could be more sensibly brought up"

dressing Elizabeth and her younger sister Margaret (born in 1930) in a simple way that implied a sensible upbringing. Likewise, as a toddler the princess was allowed to play with only a single toy at a time despite the fact that, at the age of one, she had already received three tons of toys from well-wishers. "I don't think any child could be more sensibly brought up," Queen Mary later remarked.

In fact, although a part of Antarctica was named after the young princess and a wax model of her exhibited at Madame Tussaud's, she was apparently blissfully unaware of her own exalted status. Relatives, staff and the press all insisted that her childhood was "normal", despite members of the public peering through the railings outside the family home near Green Park in central London just to catch a glimpse of the blond-haired, blue-eyed girl playing on the lawn.

During the first year of her life, Elizabeth spent six months with her paternal grandparents at Buckingham Palace while her parents went on a tour of Australia. As a result, she grew very close to the ailing King George V. The public revelled in the fact that Elizabeth apparently called him "Grandpa England", and was particularly touched when, in the winter of 1928/29, her daily visits raised his spirits so much as to help him recover from a

Opposite: A childhood portrait of Princess Elizabeth, circa 1934

*Right: Princess Elizabeth sits between
her grandparents, King George V and
Queen Mary, facing her mother, the
Duchess of York, 1932*

THE QUEEN & PRINCE PHILIP

near-fatal illness. Just over a year later, the King gave "Lilibet", as she came to be known, a pony for her fourth birthday. By that point, she had already developed her lifelong passion for horses and dogs, though she only received the first of her famous corgis for her 18th birthday.

The princess's life was transformed when, following the death of her grandfather in January 1936, his successor, her uncle, abdicated in December of that year and her father became King. Aged 10, she was suddenly first in line to the throne and therefore subject to even greater public interest. Elizabeth started to study constitutional history and law in preparation for her future role, receiving tuition from her father, as well as from Henry Marten, the Vice-Provost of Eton.

The desire for her to have a normal childhood remained. In 1937, as well as attending her father's coronation at Westminster Abbey, Elizabeth became a Girl Guide, and several years later she joined the Sea Rangers. In 1939, she travelled on the London Underground for the first time and,

Opposite: Princess Elizabeth trains as a mechanic for the Auxiliary Territorial Service, 1945

having been moved to Windsor during the Blitz, she, Princess Margaret and the children of staff members put on Christmas-time pantomime performances there. In addition, having joined the Auxiliary Territorial Service in early 1945, Princess Elizabeth learnt to drive and passed a car-maintenance course, thereby becoming the first future British monarch to be able to change a spark plug!

However, formal duties were being introduced into the teenage Elizabeth's diary, in readiness for her eventual role. She made her first radio broadcast in 1940, aged 14, was appointed Colonel-in-Chief of the Grenadier Guards in early 1942, inspected a regiment on her 16th birthday and started carrying out some of the duties of Head of State in 1944.

She turned 21 during her first state visit – a tour of southern Africa – in 1947, making a broadcast from Cape Town in which she made "a solemn act of dedication" to the Commonwealth. Not long later she would marry Philip Mountbatten at Westminster Abbey. A new chapter in her life was to begin.

"It will be for us, the children of today, to make the world of tomorrow a better and happier place"

Princess Elizabeth

The young Philip

Adversity and valour

Prince Philip's early years were both challenging and colourful, characterised by a turbulent family life and adventurous spirit that led to a successful career as a naval officer and a decorated war hero

HE MIGHT HAVE expected a life of wealth and privilege. But, despite his royal rank, Prince Philip's early life was traumatic and unorthodox, for this prince of Greece was born into volatile and dangerous times.

A great-grandson of Queen Victoria, he was born at the villa Mon Repos in Corfu on 10 June 1921. The son of a prince of Greece and Denmark, his paternal family was of Danish descent as his father, Prince Andrea (Andrew), was the grandson of King Christian IX of Denmark. His mother was Princess Alice of Battenberg, eldest child of Prince Louis of Battenberg and sister of Earl Mountbatten of Burma.

When his mother, Alice, went into labour, the doctor took her to the dining room table, which he deemed the most suitable place in the house to give birth. The baby was registered in nearby Corfu Town under the name of Philippos. The child was sixth in line to the Greek throne.

His father, a major general in the Greek army, had left for war before his son was born and it would prove to be some time before he would see his son. Indeed, the Greek military campaign in Asia Minor was a disaster, and the royal family would pay a heavy price for the resulting defeat.

Philip's father was made a scapegoat by Greece's revolutionary colonels and narrowly escaped the death sentence. His family was forced to flee the country.

Andrew, Alice, their four daughters and their 18-month-old son, Philip, escaped with no money and no travel documents. They finally settled in Paris and were supported by Prince George of Greece, Andrew's elder brother. The shock, however, took its toll. Philip's mother suffered a nervous breakdown and was eventually sectioned and institutionalised to a psychiatric clinic.

His parents then lived separate lives, with Andrew going on to live a nomadic playboy lifestyle, but still seeing his son in school holidays.

Exiled in Paris, young Philip made the best of his situation. He developed into a cheerful, occasionally truculent, but much-loved little boy. From this point on Philip went from pillar to post, left in the care of Alice's family.

"I just had to get on with it," said Philip in an interview years later. "You do. One does."

Philip's guardian for the next seven years was George, 2nd Marquess of Milford Haven, who become a great mentor to his nephew, inspiring Philip's lifelong love of design and invention.

Previous pages: Prince Philip (left) in costume for a production of Macbeth at Gordonstoun school, July 1935

Opposite: Philip as a toddler, July 1922

Left: Prince Philip (second left)
with his schoolmates in St Cloud,
France, circa 1929

"*This boy has natural qualities as a leader*"

The young prince's formal education began at The Elms infant school in the Paris suburb of St Cloud, an establishment mainly for the children of diplomats and wealthy American expatriates, with a stiffening of Royalty. Prince Philip's classmates included Prince Jacques de Bourbon and his sister Princess Anne, who later married King Michael of Romania.

At the age of eight, under the guidance of his uncle George, Philip progressed to Cheam prep school in England, where he studied from 1930 to 1933. Lynden Manor, George's house on the River Thames at Maidenhead, was Philip's home, so far as he had one at all, during the shorter school holidays.

It was George who turned up in loco parentis for the sports days and prize givings, and, on one occasion, to see Philip receive a prize for French.

In 1933, Philip was sent to Salem School in Baden, Germany, where German progressive educationalist Dr Kurt Hahn had established one of the world's best-known private schools. The school, close to Lake Constance, was also near Schloss Salem, the home of Margrave von Baden and his wife Theodora, Philip's sister.

Salem aimed to combine academic excellence with character-building, emphasising the importance of each pupil discovering his own powers. But by the time Philip arrived, Hahn had fallen foul of the Nazis, whose policies he resolutely opposed.

Hahn was imprisoned for "the decadent corruption of German youth" and only the intervention of British Prime Minister Ramsay MacDonald secured his release. He fled to Britain and founded a new school, Gordonstoun, near Elgin, Morayshire, in the Scottish Highlands, where a 13-year-old Philip became one of a handful of founding pupils.

For the next five years, Philip completed his schooling there and Gordonstoun was later chosen for all three of his sons, as well as two of his grandchildren.

Gordonstoun – which placed an emphasis on outdoor activities, particularly seamanship and expeditions – suited the student Philip. He became captain of both the school's hockey and cricket teams and was guardian (head boy)

Opposite: Philip (bottom row, centre) with members of the Gordonstoun school cricket team, circa 1938

in his last term. The headmaster noted of Philip: "This boy has natural qualities as a leader."

After leaving school, Philip joined the Royal Navy, beginning at the Britannia Royal Naval College, Dartmouth in May 1939, and was singled out as best cadet. War with Hitler's Nazi Germany was declared later that same year and in 1940 Philip was sent to sea.

As a citizen of Greece, he was initially deployed as a "neutral foreigner", serving on naval escort and convoy missions. However, after Italy invaded Greece in 1940 the young officer was assigned to Valiant, a battleship that would soon see action in the Mediterranean. Philip was commended for his operation of searchlights during a night battle near Cape Matapan in 1941, during which the British destroyed much of the Italian fleet.

A grateful fellow veteran revealed a remarkable act of heroism by Philip that saved scores of lives during the Second World War, 60 years after the incident. Harry Hargreaves recalled how quick thinking by Philip foiled a Luftwaffe bomber, which looked certain to destroy their ship during the Allied invasion of Sicily in 1943.

With the vessel under repeated bombardment, Philip came up with up a plan to throw overboard a wooden raft with smoke floats that would create the illusion of debris ablaze on the water. As he hoped, the German plane was fooled into attacking the raft while the Wallace sailed to safety under cover of darkness.

His commanding officer said: "Thanks to his alertness and appreciation of the situation, we were able to sink in five minutes two eight-inch gun Italian cruisers."

Philip was later awarded the Greek War Cross of Valour, was mentioned in dispatches and took part in the Allied landings on Sicily.

After various postings and promotions, Philip earned the rank of First Lieutenant of HMS Whelp in 1944, a destroyer that went on to see action in the Pacific as part of a British Fleet involved with joint operations with the US Navy, including the landings at Iwo Jima. He was at Tokyo Bay when the Japanese surrendered.

The prince was destined for a distinguished naval career, but fate and love would change the direction of his life forever.

Opposite: Philip, as a naval officer, inspects marines at the naval base in Corsham, Wiltshire, 1946

"The sea is an extraordinary master or mistress. It has such extraordinary moods that sometimes you feel this is the only sort of life – and then ten minutes later you're praying for death"

Prince Philip

The Royal
couple

A *blossoming* romance

From family acquaintances to courting couple, the relationship between Princess Elizabeth and Prince Philip caught the public imagination at a time of post-war hope and hardship

IT IS A romantic notion that Princess Elizabeth fell for Prince Philip at first sight, but it is not quite true. In reality, they first met, albeit fleetingly, at the wedding of Philip's cousin Princess Marina of Greece to the Duke of Kent, Elizabeth's uncle, in 1934. They were at the same function again for the coronation of George VI in 1937.

Two years later, however, the pair had a far more significant meeting on a royal visit to Dartmouth Naval College. It was in this romantic setting that the handsome and athletic Prince of Greece first caught the eye of the teenage princess.

Philip was introduced to Elizabeth at the house of the Captain of the College, later Admiral Sir Frederick Dalrymple-Hamilton, and assigned to look after her and Princess Margaret. He took the princesses to play croquet and to the tennis courts to have "some real fun jumping over the nets". The impressionable princess found Philip's good looks and free spirit appealing.

The next day, Philip and fellow cadets joined the royal party for tea. The King had hardly noticed him – until it was time for them to depart. As the royal party sailed off, a few cadets took charge of a number of small craft and set off in pursuit of the royal yacht.

The princess watched Philip through her binoculars. The King eventually spotted him and remarked, "The young fool. He must go back!" But he was certainly no fool in her eyes.

From that time on, the two maintained regular and friendly correspondence. But within a few months Philip was sent to sea. Then war with Nazi Germany was declared. Aside from fleeting visits when he was on leave, theirs was to be a romance of letters, with Philip writing to the princess from afar while at war.

Philip was always in her thoughts and when on leave the young naval officer was invited to spend Christmas 1943 with the Royal Family at Windsor.

However, stories that Philip had thoughts of marrying teenage Elizabeth when they met at Dartmouth were, according to the prince, wide of the mark.

"Well, we'd met at Dartmouth," he told biographer Basil Boothroyd, "and as far as I was concerned it was a very amusing experience, going on board the yacht and meeting them, and that sort of thing, and that was that.

"Elizabeth began to play the tune 'People Will Say We're in Love'"

Opening pages: Princess Elizabeth and Philip, 1947

Previous pages: Arriving at the Royal Naval College in Dartmouth in 1939 – Prince Philip, Princess Margaret, Queen Elizabeth, King George VI and Princess Elizabeth

Opposite: Elizabeth, at the wedding of Patricia Mountbatten and Baron Brabourne, with her father, sister, mother and Philip, 1946

"Then I went to – did I go to Windsor? I think I came here to Buckingham Palace. Or I went to the theatre with them once, something like that. And then, during the war, if I was here, I'd call in and have a meal. I once or twice spent Christmas at Windsor, because I'd nowhere particular to go … I thought not all that much about it, I think.

"We used to correspond occasionally. I suppose if I'd just been a casual acquaintance it would all have been frightfully significant. But if you're related … it isn't so extraordinary to be on kind of family-relationship terms with somebody. You don't necessarily have to think about marriage.

"I suppose one thing led to another. I suppose I began to think about it seriously when I got back in '46 and went to Balmoral. It was probably then that we began to think about it seriously and even talk about it."

Philip arrived back from the Far East with his destroyer HMS Whelp in January 1946. A series of unexciting home postings had left him restless and disillusioned after the excitement of action. In a letter to Elizabeth, he admitted he was "still not accustomed to the idea of peace, rather fed up with everything and feeling that there was not much to look forward to and rather grudgingly accepting the idea of going on in the peacetime navy."

His postings had a positive side, however, and meant he could make frequent trips to London. Marion Crawford, Elizabeth's governess, described seeing Philip's black, green-upholstered MG sports car roaring into the forecourt of Buckingham Palace and the prince getting out "hatless" and "always in a hurry to see Lilibet". Elizabeth began to take more trouble with her appearance and to play the tune "People Will Say We're in Love" from the musical Oklahoma.

In London, Philip would stay either with his grandmother, Princess Victoria, at Kensington Palace or on a camp bed at the home of his uncle, Dickie Mountbatten. In visitors' books

*Left: Elizabeth and Philip wave
at cheering crowds as they leave
Buckingham Palace on 10 July, 1947,
shortly after the announcement of
their engagement*

Opposite: Princess Elizabeth (left)
with Philip, Queen Elizabeth, King
George VI and Princess Margaret at
Buckingham Palace, October 1947

at the time, he declared himself "of no fixed abode". But wherever he laid his head, in his bag was a photograph of Princess Elizabeth in a battered leather frame.

On 29 May 1946, Philip was photographed standing next to Elizabeth at the wedding of her new lady-in-waiting but was described in the press as "a figure largely unknown to the British public".

They tried to avoid being seen together and, if they were in the same party, took the precaution of not dancing with each other. But in reality, the courtship was serious.

When news of the royal romance reached the press, it was Elizabeth's first experience of a new kind of public interest. Her personal life had become public property. When she turned up at engagements, people in the crowd would shout, "Where's Philip?"

In June 1946, Philip wrote to Elizabeth apologising for the "monumental cheek" of having invited himself to the Palace. "Yet however contrite I feel," he wrote, "there is always a small voice that keeps saying 'nothing ventured, nothing gained' – well did I venture and I gained a wonderful time." Late that summer, Elizabeth asked him to Balmoral for three weeks to shoot grouse and stalk. It was there that he is understood to have proposed.

Philip applied for British nationality and, in February 1947, became a naturalised British subject, renouncing his Greek royal title and adopting the surname of Mountbatten. Everything was now in place for them to seal their love with a royal marriage.

My husband and I...

Despite having to contend with a time of austerity and rationing, the nation put on a grand show for the wedding of the future Queen and her dashing war-hero husband

IT WAS THE glittering Royal Wedding that lit up the post-war gloom of Britain. On a cold but dry winter day – 20 November 1947 – thousands of excited well-wishers packed solid from Buckingham Palace to Westminster Abbey, all desperate to catch a glimpse of the Princess bride and her dashing groom. Even Trafalgar Square was full to the fountains.

The engagement had been officially announced once the 21-year-old Princess Elizabeth had returned from a tour of South Africa – although she had become secretly engaged to her love the Royal Naval officer Lieutenant Philip Mountbatten a year earlier, after he had proposed to the future Queen during a walk around the grounds of Balmoral in Scotland.

Their engagement had remained hidden from the public for a year because the King was against her marrying at such a young age. But when the time was right, a court circular was issued from Buckingham Palace making the announcement. "The King has gladly given his consent," it read.

The following day, Elizabeth and Philip had made their first joint public appearance at a Palace garden party, with the excited princess proudly wearing her platinum and diamond engagement ring, made by jeweller Philip Antrobus using diamonds from a tiara that had belonged to her fiancé's mother.

Lord Beaverbrook's Daily Express trumpeted: "Today the British people, turning aside from the anxieties of a time of troubles, find hope as well as joy in the royal romance." Everyone in the nation, it seemed, had fallen in love with the royal couple and their romantic story. For, despite Philip's ancestry – he and The Queen are third cousins and share Queen Victoria as a great-great- grandmother – this was not a dynastic marriage of convenience, but a triumph of love, romance and trust.

The royal carriages were buffed to a high gloss; the Life Guards and Household Cavalry, plumed and burnished, and deployed; flags, banners and bunting were on display, too. Inside Westminster Abbey, the Lords of the Church assembled, attending robed royals were present too – including the King and Queen of Denmark, the King and Queen of Yugoslavia, the Kings of Norway and Romania, and the Shah of Iran. All waited patiently, along with 2,000 other guests, for the arrival of the beautiful bride.

"The occasion was watched by thousands at packed cinemas across the country"

Opening pages: Elizabeth and Philip pose with family members and foreign nobility after their wedding

Previous pages: Philip sets off from Kensington Palace on the day of his wedding

Opposite: Princess Elizabeth and her father King George VI arrive at Westminster Abbey

The occasion was filmed by camera crews and later watched by thousands at packed cinemas across the country. A further 200 million people around the world listened to the ceremony on their radio. This was a truly global event, captivating millions across the Empire and beyond. Over 10,000 telegrams were sent to Buckingham Palace to congratulations the couple from, among others, France's Charles de Gaulle, the Mayor of Sutton Coldfield and the Chinese Navy.

As the New York Times recorded, the wedding was a, "welcome occasion for gaiety in grim England, beset in peace with troubles almost as burdensome as those of the war." This was the first great state occasion in the post-war years and a distraction from the real hardships the British people were facing in the aftermath of the Second World War.

Not everyone was enthused, however. Among the dissenting voices was the Camden Town First Branch of the Amalgamated Society of Woodworkers. Buoyant on the tide of the first Labour government since 1929, they wrote direct to His Majesty the King warning that, "any banqueting and display of wealth at your daughter's wedding will be an insult to the British people at the present time, and we consider that you would be well advised to order a very quiet wedding in keeping with the times".

The disgruntled missive went on, "May we also remind you that should you declare the wedding day a public holiday you will have a word beforehand with the London Master Builders' Association to ensure that we are paid for it."

The letter did nothing to dampen the King's mood. Princess Elizabeth's wedding dress, designed for her by Norman Hartnell, was breathtaking. However, given that the rationing of clothing was still in place at the time, she famously saved up her ration cards to purchase the material needed for her wedding gown.

In another nod to the austere times, the two royal kneelers used during the service were made from orange boxes covered in rose pink silk, due to wartime austerity.

Left: King George VI gives away his daughter at Westminster Abbey, in a service conducted by the Archbishop of Canterbury, Geoffrey Fisher

Elizabeth's wedding dress was a triumph. It was decorated with more than 10,000 white pearls imported from America, silver thread and tulle embroidery. The fabric for the dress was woven at Winterthur Silks Limited, Dunfermline, in the Canmore factory, using silk that had come from Chinese silkworms at Lullingstone Castle.

The Queen's bridal veil was made of tulle and held by a tiara of diamonds that was originally made for Queen Mary from re-used diamonds taken from jewellery purchased by Queen Victoria from Collingwood and Co. The spreading skirt of ivory Duchesse satin, below a fitted bodice with heart-shaped neckline and long tight sleeves, was embroidered with garlands of roses in raised pearls entwined with ears of wheat in crystals and pearls.

Round the full hem, a border of orange blossom was appliquéd with transparent tulle, outlined in seed pearls and crystals. The fan-shaped train, 15-feet-long, in transparent ivory silk tulle, ended in a deep border of embroidered roses and wheat motifs.

At her wedding, Elizabeth – whose wedding ring was made from the same nugget of Welsh gold from Clogau St David's, Bontddu, North Wales as her mother's ring – had eight bridesmaids and two pages. Her sister Princess Margaret led the bridesmaids – Princess Alexandra, Lady Caroline Montagu-Douglas-Scott, Lady Mary Cambridge,

Lady Elizabeth Lambart, Pamela Mountbatten, Margaret Elphinstone and Diana Bowes-Lyon. The two pages, her cousins Prince William of Gloucester and Prince Michael of Kent, were both aged just five.

The bride's wedding bouquet – white orchids with a sprig of myrtle from the bush grown from the original myrtle in Queen Victoria's wedding bouquet – was supplied by the Worshipful Company of Gardeners and arranged by the florist MH Longman. An identical copy of the bouquet was made and presented to The Queen on her Golden Wedding in 1997.

The grave of the Unknown Warrior was the only stone that was not covered by the special carpet in the abbey, and the day after the wedding, Princess Elizabeth followed a royal tradition started by her mother, of sending her wedding bouquet back to the abbey to be laid there.

The couple received more than 2,500 wedding presents from well-wishers around the world. Most of the gifts were put on display for a few days in a charity exhibition at St James's Palace, which was attended by over 200,000 visitors.

The official wedding cake was made by McVities and Price, although 11 other cakes were given as presents. Due to post-war food rationing, ingredients were sent as wedding presents from overseas. The official cake, which stood nine feet high in four tiers with painted panels of the armorial bearings of both families, was made using ingredients given as a wedding gift by the Australian Girl

Crowds watch the Irish State Coach as it travels along The Mall, accompanied by a sovereign's escort of the Household Cavalry

Left: The royal group on the balcony of Buckingham Palace after returning from Westminster Abbey, including Elizabeth's bridesmaids, Philip's best man the Marquis of Milford-Haven, page boy and cousin to the princess Prince William of Gloucester, and the bride and groom

"The princess wrote that she and Philip 'behave as though we had belonged to each other for years'"

Guides. It also included the monograms of bride and groom.

The King was deeply moved by the experience. In an emotional letter he wrote to his daughter afterwards, he said, "I was so proud of you and thrilled at having you so close to me on our long walk in Westminster Abbey, but when I handed your hand to the Archbishop I felt that I had lost something very precious."

Elizabeth was in heaven. In a letter to her parents, the princess wrote that she and Philip "behave as though we had belonged to each other for years," adding: "Philip is an angel – he is so kind and thoughtful."

Their ambition for their marriage, she added, was to weld themselves into a "combined existence" able to withstand the shocks directed at them but "also have a positive existence for the good".

The King, who was in frail health, had reason to be concerned. He knew it would not be long before these two young people would have to face the challenge of leadership.

"I wonder if Philip knows what he is taking on," George VI confided prophetically to a guest at the wedding breakfast held in the Ball Supper Room at Buckingham Palace, at which the menu was Filet de Sole Mountbatten, Perdreau en Casserole (a braised partridge dish) and Bombe Glacee Princess Elizabeth. "One day Lilibet will be queen and he will be consort. That's much harder than being a king, but I think he's the man for the job," he added.

The couple honeymooned at Broadlands, the Mountbatten family home in Hampshire, and at Birkhall on the Balmoral estate in Scotland. On their return, they moved into Buckingham Palace as a temporary residence until their marital home, Clarence House, was ready.

Within five years the King's words would prove prophetic. He would be dead and it would fall on Philip to break the terrible news to his young wife. However, throughout his long and extraordinary life, Philip has lived up to the King's expectations and has certainly proved he was the man for the job; Her Majesty's "Liege Man".

Opposite: The Royal couple pose together shortly after their wedding

Crowning glory

The enthronement of a new sovereign is an occasion for both solemnity and celebration, and for The Queen and The Duke of Edinburgh, the Coronation's display of ceremony, regalia and fanfare was no exception

Previous pages: The Queen and The Duke of Edinburgh wave to the crowds from the balcony at Buckingham Palace

Opposite: Philip pays humble and dutiful homage to his wife Queen Elizabeth II as part of the Coronation ceremony

PRINCESS ELIZABETH ASCENDED to the throne on 6 February 1952, upon the death of her father, King George VI, and was proclaimed Queen shortly afterwards by assorted privy councils and executives. However, there would be a lengthy gap of 16 months between her accession and the Coronation.

This delay was partly due to the tradition that the celebratory nature of a coronation is inappropriate during the mourning period that follows the death of a monarch. Queen Victoria, for example, became monarch on the death of King William IV on 20 June 1837 but was not crowned until the following June, and other Hanoverian coronations observed this custom. The exception was Her Majesty The Queen's father, King George VI, as his predecessor King Edward VIII did not die but abdicated. Princess Elizabeth watched that coronation, on 12 May 1937, as an 11-year-old girl.

However, in a country that was still recovering from the devastating effects of war, the delay provided time to organise a suitably grand ceremony. A Coronation Commission was set up in April 1952, chaired by The Duke of Edinburgh, while the Coronation Joint Committee was established to coordinate foreign visits. The event was organised by The Duke of Norfolk, Bernard Fitzalan-Howard, who was also in charge of King George VI's coronation, and would go on to organise Sir Winston Churchill's funeral in 1965 and Prince Charles's investiture in 1969.

The Coronation took place in Westminster Abbey on 2 June 1953. It was a dignified ceremony conducted by Dr Geoffrey Fisher, Archbishop of Canterbury, which began at 11.15 am and concluded at 2 pm. The service was divided into six parts – the recognition, the oath, the anointing, the investiture (which included the crowning), the enthronement and the homage. The anointing had a particular significance, using an anointing liquid made from the oils of orange, rose, cinnamon, musk and ambergris.

"A total of 8,251 guests were present, the youngest being the four-and-a-half-year-old Prince Charles"

During the investiture, The Queen put on a robe of cloth of gold (the Dalmatic, which was used by King George VI) and was presented with golden spurs, a jewelled sword and golden bracelets. Finally, she put on the Imperial Mantle and received the Orb, the Coronation Ring, the Coronation Glove and two sceptres. Music, directed by abbey organist William McKie and performed by 480 musicians and singers, included settings of Handel's "Zadok the Priest" and Hubert Parry's "I Was Glad", and new compositions by Ralph Vaughan Williams, Arnold Bax, William Walton and the Canadian composer Healy Willan.

A total of 8,251 guests were present, the youngest being the four-and-a-half-year-old Prince Charles. Prime Minister Winston Churchill – who had started his second spell in Downing Street in 1951 – was joined by representatives of 129 countries, with Commonwealth prime ministers including India's Jawaharlal Nehru, Australia's Robert Menzies, Canada's Louis Saint-Laurent, Pakistan's Muhammad Ali Bogra and South Africa's D F Malan.

Tradition dictates that a queen consort is crowned with a king in a similar, somewhat simpler, ceremony, but that if the new sovereign is a queen, her consort is not crowned or

Opposite: Queen Elizabeth II walks down the nave in Westminster Abbey after being crowned

Right: Crowds brave the rain to line around Pall Mall and Trafalgar Square in central London to watch Queen Elizabeth II as she tours the city after her Coronation at Westminster Abbey

"*Many people bought their first televisions to watch the event, and dozens crowded around each set*"

Opposite: The newly crowned Queen Elizabeth II and The Duke of Edinburgh in the State Coach, just after the Coronation

anointed at the coronation. However, after The Queen was crowned, The Duke of Edinburgh was the first, after the attending archbishops and bishops, to pay homage to her.

Following the ceremony, The Queen and The Duke of Edinburgh were then driven back from Westminster Abbey to Buckingham Palace in the Gold State Coach, which was pulled by eight grey geldings: Cunningham, Tovey, Noah, Tedder, Eisenhower, Snow White, Tipperary and McCreery.

The two-hour return procession took a deliberately convoluted five-mile route – via Whitehall, Trafalgar Square, Pall Mall, Hyde Park Corner, Marble Arch and Oxford Circus – and was lined by 29,000 troops from Britain and the Commonwealth. Hundreds of thousands of people viewed the procession all along the route, despite heavy rain. Many even camped for two days in prime positions in order to get a good view. One Australian family had sailed all the way to London in a ketch to witness the spectacle.

The ceremony was also broadcast on radio around the world and, at The Queen's request, on television for the first time – a breakthrough in outside broadcasting. Many people bought their first televisions to watch the event, and dozens crowded around each set. Given that the population of the UK was around 36 million at the time, it's estimated that 27 million watched the event on television, and a further 11 million listened on the radio. More than 2,000 journalists and 500 photographers from around the world covered the event – including one Jacqueline Bouvier, later to be First Lady Jackie Kennedy, then a correspondent for the Washington Times-Herald.

On the day of the Coronation, the Royal Family also received the news that New Zealand-born mountaineer Edmund Hillary and the Nepalese Sherpa Tenzing Norgay had become the first people to reach the summit of Mount Everest, an achievement that was described as the ultimate coronation gift to The Queen.

Opposite: Queen Elizabeth II with The Duke of Edinburgh, Princess Margaret, Queen Elizabeth The Queen Mother and members of the immediate and extended Royal Family in the Throne Room of Buckingham Palace

> *"Princess Elizabeth was enamoured from an early age. She never looked at anyone else. She was smitten from the start"*

Margaret Rhodes on her cousin The Queen

The Queen
& The Duke

Duty and devotion

Over the past seven decades,
The Queen and Prince Philip's
deep sense of duty has helped make
Britain's state occasions and official
engagements the envy of the world

"**AND WHAT HAVE** kings that privates have not too, save ceremony… gorgeous ceremony?" asks Shakespeare's Henry V as he wanders, disguised as a soldier in order to comfort his men, on the eve of Agincourt.

It is precisely that "gorgeous ceremony", concluded the great Victorian constitutionalist, Walter Bagehot, some 450 years later, that gives the monarchy its "magic", the "mystery [that] is its life".

From Trooping the Colour to the State Opening of Parliament or the Garter Service, no other nation has retained the same degree of devotion and respect for these ancient ceremonies, embodied in the State Carriage processions that convey the Royal Family to many of their duties.

Her Majesty The Queen and The Duke of Edinburgh's year is demarcated by such engagements, and these are not only the magnificent and high-profile events. There are also the many Investitures (knighthoods, MBEs, OBEs and various Orders of Chivalry and Orders of Merit) that honour the achievements of individuals who have served their communities; as well as the Garden Parties, which acknowledge the public service of people from all walks of life.

There is the fun and festivity of Royal Ascot, which begins each day with the Royal Procession, and then there is the sombre and the humble; The Queen and Prince Philip leading the laying of wreaths at The Cenotaph on Remembrance Day and distributing the Maundy money to pensioners during Easter week.

These events are legion: a typical year sees some 25 Investitures and usually two State Visits hosted by The Queen, with the attendant ceremonial welcome, Guard of Honour and State Banquet for the visiting Head of State. There will be at least three Garden Parties at Buckingham Palace and another at the Palace of Holyroodhouse in Edinburgh, with 8,000 to 10,000 guests at each one.

Among the most colourful ceremonies are the State Opening of Parliament in early summer, Trooping the Colour – to mark The

Opening pages: Her Majesty and The Duke of Edinburgh with Prince Charles (left) and Princess Anne (right) at the State Opening of Parliament, 1967

Previous pages: The Queen rides alongside Philip at Trooping The Colour, 1983

Opposite: The Royal couple attend the annual service for the Order of the Garter at Windsor, 1985

Queen's official birthday, in June – and the annual procession and Order of the Garter Service at Windsor, the oldest British Order of Chivalry, founded by Edward III in 1348. These ceremonies, according to the Royal historian and commentator Rafe Heydel-Mankoo, "connect us to our justifiably proud heritage and are admired across the globe". Such is the importance of the Royal Family's ceremonial duties that during her reign, The Queen has missed only two State Openings of Parliament (in 1959 and 1963, due to pregnancy) and four Maundy ceremonies.

The Royal couple have also taken part in hundreds of military ceremonies over the years. Both have served in the military: Her Majesty, while Princess Elizabeth, donned a uniform in the Auxiliary Territorial Service as an engine mechanic and driver, while Prince Philip had a distinguished naval career, rising to the rank of lieutenant and being mentioned in dispatches and decorated for bravery during the Second World War. The Queen is, of course, Commander-in-Chief, while The Duke of Edinburgh has numerous titles – including Admiral of the Fleet of the Royal Navy, Field Marshal and Marshal of the RAF and Captain-General of the Royal Marines. He is also Colonel or Colonel-in-Chief of many British and overseas regiments. In these roles, each year the Royal couple will visit many specific regiments, ships or military bases, while also receiving visitors from the British Armed Forces.

The Queen continues to be supported in her duties by The Duke of Edinburgh and by other members of the Royal Family, as she has throughout her reign. The Prince of Wales, The Princess Royal and The Duke of Cambridge often hold Investitures on behalf of The Queen. Her Majesty is also represented on overseas tours by members of the Royal Family, which we see in The Duke and Duchess of Cambridge's recent visit to Poland and Germany, and Prince Harry's visit in October to Denmark.

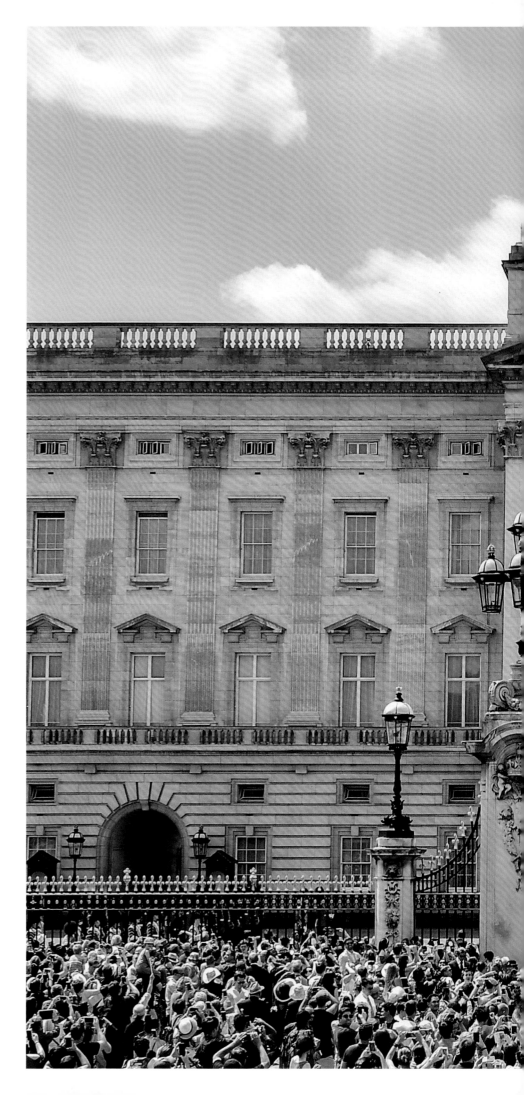

Right: The Royal Family and assembled crowds watch the Red Arrows fly over Buckingham Palace during Trooping the Colour, 2017

"The Duke is still patron, president or member of 780 organisations"

Opposite: As Captain General of the Royal Marines, Prince Philip attends a parade to mark the finale of the 1664 Global Challenge at Buckingham Palace – his last official engagement – in August 2017

At the age of 91, The Queen's engagements remain as numerous as ever – 341 in 2015, according to the Court Circular, the official record of Royal duties. Although there are no such figures for engagements throughout The Queen's historic 65-year reign, that number will be in the tens of thousands.

In May 2017, Prince Philip – not long before his 96th birthday – announced that he would be retiring from public engagements from the autumn. His last solo official engagement was receiving the Royal Marines at Buckingham Palace in August 2017. It was his 22,219th solo engagement, almost 70 years after his first one on 2 March 1948, where he attended the London Federation of Boys' Club Boxing finals at the Royal Albert Hall. He is still patron, president or member of more than 780 organisations, with which he will continue to be associated. Although he will no longer be playing an active role in attending engagements, he is likely to continue to attend many events alongside The Queen from time to time.

In an ever-changing, fast-moving world, the tradition and symbolism of ceremonial and State occasions ensure continuity, stability and national pride. "There is nothing to match the panoply of State," says the Crown Equerry, Colonel Toby Browne, the man responsible for the Royal Mews and those glorious carriage processions.

That "gorgeous ceremony" as evoked by Shakespeare and embodied in a State carriage procession with its attendant escort, "is one of the factors," says Colonel Browne, "that ensures Great Britain remains unequalled in the modern world in terms of ceremonial pageantry".

A world of welcomes

In their lives of faithful service to Britain and the Commonwealth, the Royal couple have travelled to every corner of the earth, extending the hand of friendship and diplomacy around the globe

DESPITE HER MAJESTY The Queen not possessing a passport, she and her consort The Duke of Edinburgh are one of the most well-travelled couples on earth. She's the undisputed Royal record holder for globetrotting, having visited 128 countries during her long reign, many of them several times.

"When anyone refers to 'The Queen' they immediately think of Elizabeth II," says author and Royal editor of the Evening Standard Robert Jobson. "She is the most famous person on the planet, a global icon. Not only The Queen of Great Britain but of Australia, Canada, New Zealand and all the realms and dominions, and Head of the Commonwealth."

Trips to places where she is Queen are known as "Royal visits"; tours to other countries are "State visits". On every trip she has been accompanied by The Duke of Edinburgh. Whether a subject of Her Majesty or not, seeing or meeting The Queen is an unforgettable experience. As such, a great deal of thought goes into itineraries to ensure as many as possible have this opportunity. This adds another dimension to planning The Queen's wardrobe to make her visible amid large crowds.

The first "walkabout" took place during the 1970 Australia and New Zealand tour. Up until this point, seeing The Queen and Prince Philip at close quarters had been the preserve of dignitaries and officials. Perhaps it was apt that the focus shifted towards meeting the masses given her ascent to the throne coincided with the dawn of the television age. The world could not get enough of the beautiful young Queen and her consort when they embarked on their tour of the Commonwealth in 1953 – the first

Previous spread: The Royal couple in Addis Ababa, Ethiopia, 1965

Opposite: The Queen and The Duke of Edinburgh are carried in a canoe on a tour in Tuvalu, 1982

"Photographs of the Royal couple's travels act as a window into faraway lands and cultures"

Opposite: The Queen, accompanied by various Ashanti chieftains and President Kwame Nkrumah, during a visit to Ghana, 1961

Left: The Queen and Prince Philip
are presented with a bouquet on
their arrival in Barbados, 1966

on HMS Britannia, who would accrue over a million miles
during her service.

Footage and photographs of the Royal couple's travels
have given us not only a window into faraway lands and
other cultures but also glimpses of Her Majesty the tourist,
foot tapping to joyful traditional dances or carrying a
camera around her neck like any other sightseer.

The exchange of official gifts is an important part of
such visits. These have included a marzipan Brandenburg
Gate, presented during her latest trip to Germany, and a pair
of cowboy boots given to Her Majesty when she toured the
USA in 1991. Among the most unusual gifts are live animals:
the most exotic of these, which have included sloths, jaguars,
an elephant and giant turtles, have been homed in London
Zoo. The Queen has also received a number of horses,
including Burmese the striking black mare given to her
by the Royal Canadian Mounted Police and ridden by Her
Majesty at Trooping the Colour until 1986.

Canada is the country most visited by The Queen during her reign. She has described it as her "second home", and her affection for the country and its people is evident. Modern communications have allowed visits by the Royal Family on a near yearly basis, and it surprised few that The Duke and Duchess of Cambridge visited Canada for their first official overseas tour together.

These official visits by The Queen and Prince Philip play an important role in cementing relationships between the UK and other countries. In doing so, Her Majesty has registered significant "firsts", including being the first reigning British Monarch to make State visits to China, Russia, Brunei, Malaysia and South Korea. These trips can have added significance in the aftermath of a natural disaster or significant event, such as the visit to flood-ravaged Brisbane in 2011 or the 1995 State visit to South Africa following the end of apartheid.

One of the most important events occurred in 2011 when The Queen travelled to Ireland. It was the first visit by a British monarch to the republic in a century and marked a huge milestone in relations between the two countries. "The Queen made a very positive impact, especially with her visit to our national independence memorial and the powerful message of reconciliation she incorporated into her speeches," says Irish Ambassador to London Daniel Mulhall. "She was well received by the Irish people and her visit left a lasting impression."

According to Robert Jobson, The Queen's influence should never be underestimated. "As the longest-reigning British Monarch, it has spanned many decades," he says. "She has touched the lives of leaders from Churchill and Kennedy to Reagan and Thatcher, as well as the millions of people she has met as she travels the world. Elizabeth II is a global phenomenon, the like of which I don't think we will see again. She has dedicated her life to service and duty, serving with humility and steadfastness the institution of Monarchy that she heads."

Opposite: The Royal couple at a civic ceremony in New Delhi during the Royal Tour of India, 1961

Left: The Queen and Prince Philip arrive at Ciampino Airport in Rome, en route to a State visit to the Vatican in 2014

Happy and glorious

Having reigned for longer than any other British monarch, The Queen has been the focus for a host of national celebrations, from jubilees to birthdays to this latest landmark wedding anniversary

Previous pages: The Queen arrives at her star-studded 90th birthday celebration, accompanied by Prince Philip, 2016

Opposite: The Royal couple sort through cables of congratulations on the morning of their Silver Wedding anniversary, 1972

HER MAJESTY'S MARRIAGE to The Duke of Edinburgh has been the foundation of every aspect of her life. Throughout, Prince Philip has helped her steer the monarchy from a time of imperial power into a multicultural, multimedia age; from the uncertainty of the end of Empire to the new burgeoning Commonwealth.

They may not be a couple who show their emotions publicly but on their Golden Wedding Anniversary in November 1997, The Queen put her feelings on record. "Prince Philip is someone who doesn't take easily to compliments but he has, quite simply, been my strength and stay all these years. And I owe him a debt greater than he would ever claim, or we shall ever know," she said.

Together they have travelled more than any other British monarch and consort. Her Majesty has lived longer and reigned longer than any of her predecessors too, surpassing Queen Victoria's record as the longest-reigning monarch in 2015.

When the moment came to mark that record she ruled out any staged major celebration. She thanked well wishers at home and abroad for their "touching messages of kindness". The then British Prime Minister, David Cameron, described her service as monarch as "truly humbling".

Her Majesty's reign has been peppered with major milestones and public celebrations. In July 1969, she installed the 20-year-old Prince Charles as the Prince of Wales at Caernarvon Castle. Charles swore to be her "liege man of life and limb" during the ceremony.

Four years later, in November 1973, the focus was on her 23-year-old daughter when hundreds of thousands turned out to cheer on the marriage of Princess Anne to army officer Mark Phillips at Westminster Abbey.

The Queen celebrated her Silver Jubilee in 1977 and, despite initial mutterings among the public about cost, the historic anniversary aroused strong feelings of loyalty among the people. Across Britain, millions took the day off and celebrated with their own street parties.

During a speech, The Queen said, movingly, "When I was 21, I pledged my life to the service

Right: The Queen laughs with a crowd of children during a Silver Jubilee walkabout in 1977

"Her Majesty's reign has been peppered with major milestones and public celebrations"

of our people and asked for God's help to make good that vow. Although that vow was made in my salad days, when I was green in judgment, I do not regret nor retract one word of it."

In July 1981, the world watched in awe the "fairy-tale" wedding of Prince Charles and Lady Diana Spencer. A 600,000-strong crowd filled the streets of London to catch a glimpse of the couple as they made their way to St Paul's Cathedral to exchange their vows. Around 750 million more people viewed it on television all over the world, making it the most watched broadcast ever.

Along with the ups, there have been downs as well. In 1992, The Queen experienced one of the most difficult periods of her reign. It saw the break-up of three royal marriages – the separations of Prince Charles and Princess Diana, and the Duke and Duchess of York, and the divorce of Princess Anne and Captain Mark Phillips.

Perhaps the most challenging moment in The Queen's reign came with the death of Diana, Princess of Wales in August 1997. As millions mourned the "people's princess", a ground swell of public ill-feeling was directed towards the monarchy. The Queen's decision to remain in Balmoral to protect her grieving grandsons had left those gathered in London angry and confused.

Opposite: Her Majesty commemorates her upcoming Golden Jubilee year celebrations with Prince Philip at Buckingham Palace, 2001

Left: The Queen and The Duke of Edinburgh celebrate their Diamond Wedding Anniversary in 2007 at Broadlands in Hampshire – the former home of Prince Philip's uncle Earl Mountbatten – where the couple spent their wedding night

Right: The Royal couple arrive at Chelsea Pier in readiness for the Thames Diamond Jubilee Pageant to celebrate the 60th anniversary of Her Majesty's accession, 2012

When they returned to London on the eve of the funeral, The Queen and Prince Philip were applauded as they mingled with the crowd and inspected the enormous display of floral tributes. The Queen later delivered a dignified televised address and paid a moving tribute to Diana.

Her Majesty welcomed in the new century at the Millennium Dome with a chorus of "Auld Lang Syne" alongside Tony Blair and his wife Cherie. The nation celebrated Queen Elizabeth, The Queen Mother becoming a centenarian in the summer of 2000, making her the first member of the Royal Family to reach her 100th birthday.

The Queen suffered a terrible double loss in March 2002. First, her sister, Princess Margaret, died and then her mother passed away peacefully in her sleep at the age of 101. It was a terrible way to start The Queen's Golden Jubilee year, but sadness turned to joy when, in June, millions took to the streets to cheer Her Majesty.

Once again, The Queen paid tribute to her husband, this time during her Golden Jubilee speech at the Guildhall. "The Duke of Edinburgh has made an invaluable contribution to my life over these past 50 years," she said.

"The Queen and Prince Philip were applauded as they mingled with the crowd and inspected the display of floral tributes"

In April 2005, Prince Charles married his long-term love Camilla Parker Bowles at Windsor's Guildhall. Afterwards, the couple returned to St George's Chapel, led by the Archbishop of Canterbury Dr Rowan Williams. In November 2007, The Queen and Prince Philip marked their Diamond Wedding Anniversary.

Prince William and Catherine Middleton married in 2011, with around a million well-wishers lining the London streets and some 34 million viewers tuning in to watch the ceremony throughout the UK, joined by a further 25 million in the USA.

The Queen's Diamond Jubilee in 2012 was a chance for her people to look back as well as forward. On an unexpectedly chilly June day, The Queen's Thames Diamond Jubilee Pageant came to a close as a world record-beating 1,000-strong flotilla passed under Tower Bridge.

A 41-gun salute was fired from the Tower of London to celebrate The Queen's 60 years on the throne, accompanied by the cheers of the thousands of people gathered. The bascules of Tower Bridge opened for the arrival of the royal barge, The Spirit of Chartwell, as The Queen and Prince Philip sailed under it, accompanied by the Prince of Wales, the Duchess of Cornwall, the Duke and Duchess of Cambridge, and Prince Harry.

Unfortunately, The Duke of Edinburgh was taken ill after the pageant and had to miss much of the planned Jubilee celebrations. Four days of Diamond Jubilee events culminated in an appearance by The Queen on the Buckingham Palace balcony in front of huge, cheering crowds.

More recently still, Her Majesty's 90th birthday party was held in the grounds of Windsor Castle in 2016. A celebration of The Queen's life, dedication to the Commonwealth and international affairs, and deep involvement with the armed forces, the five-day event provided those attending and millions of television viewers worldwide with the opportunity to herald a monarch who, without overstepping her constitutional boundaries, has proved to be a unifying force for good.

Opposite: The Queen and the Duke on The Mall, welcoming more than 10,000 guests to the Patron's Lunch in 2016. The event celebrated the work of 600 charities and organisations

"He has, quite simply, been my strength and stay all these years, and I, and his whole family, and this and many other countries, owe him a debt greater than he would ever claim, or we shall ever know"

The Queen on Prince Philip

Elizabeth
& Philip

A *lifelong* passion

The Queen and Prince Philip share an avid love of all things equestrian, be it the Duke's polo playing and carriage driving, or Her Majesty's devotion to horse riding

THE QUEEN AND The Duke of Edinburgh's far-reaching influence on the horse world is the continuance of a royal tradition that follows the founding of the Royal Stud at Hampton Court in the 16th century, King Charles ll moving his court to Newmarket every year and Queen Anne spotting the potential for a racecourse at Ascot.

Whatever the occasion – whether inspecting the showing lines at Royal Windsor, arriving to cheers at Royal Ascot, watching their family play polo or seeing Prince Philip taking part in a carriage-driving event – the Royal couple have lent a gravitas and expertise to the British equestrian scene that is the envy of the rest of the world.

Early photographs show a young Princess Elizabeth sitting confidently on a black Shetland pony, Peggy, a fourth birthday present, and she and Princess Margaret were sent to learn to ride and drive with riding instructor Horace Smith and his daughter Sybil in Maidenhead. In 1945, the princesses won the private turnout (driving) class at Royal Windsor Horse Show with their pony Hans, and the show remains an annual diary date.

The Queen's father, grandfather and great-grandfather owned racehorses – King Edward Vll was the last monarch to have a Derby winner (his home-bred Persimmon in 1896) and his horses were trained at Kingsclere in Hampshire, where Her Majesty currently has some of her 25 or so racehorses in training with Andrew Balding.

The Queen inherited King George Vl's flat racehorses (her mother had the jumpers). Her ownership got off to a thrilling and, no doubt, pleasantly distracting start when Aureole finished second in the Derby just days after the Coronation.

The distinctive royal racing colours – purple, gold and red with a black velvet hat with gold fringe – have been carried to victory more than 800 times, and The Queen was leading owner in the 1950s before the might of Middle Eastern-owned horsepower began to dominate. The Derby is the only classic race that The Queen has yet to win – her last runner, Carlton House, a gift from Sheikh Mohammed al Maktoum, was sent off favourite in 2011 and finished third.

Previous pages: Her Majesty surveys a distant Balmoral Castle during the Royal Family's annual summer holiday, 1971

Opposite: Princess Elizabeth rides her pony in Windsor Great Park in the mid 1930s

"The Queen often visits her horses and is knowledgeable about bloodlines"

In 2013, The Queen was named Racehorse Owner of the Year for her contribution to the sport and in recognition of her first Ascot Gold Cup winner, Estimate, trained by Sir Michael Stoute. It was her first Grade One winner since Dunfermline, winner of the Epsom Oaks in 1977, and pictures of a delighted monarch were beamed around the world.

The Queen sets aside diary time every year to visit her horses in training and is hugely knowledgeable about bloodlines. She stands two stallions at the Royal Stud at Sandringham, Royal Applause and the Derby winner Motivator, which was bought by The Queen's racing manager, John Warren.

The Queen is an elegant, competent horsewoman, as was demonstrated in a terrifying moment during Trooping the Colour in 1981 when blank shots were fired from the crowd. The result could have been disastrous, but The Queen quietly reassured her mount, Burmese, and all was well. Burmese was a much-loved sight; a gift in 1969 from the Royal Canadian Mounted Police, the horse carried The Queen a remarkable 18 times at Trooping

the Colour. She has also followed eventing ever since Badminton Horse Trials was started by the 10th Duke of Beaufort in 1949; her annual visit would include hacking out with the Duke and Princess Margaret and watching the cross-country from a rug beside the lake with the rest of the crowd.

Her Majesty and The Duke of Edinburgh clearly share a love of equestrian sports. Prince Philip was an enthusiastic polo player from his teens, and became a regular player at the Windsor Park Polo Club for more than two decades. That was until 1971 when, aged 50, an arthritic wrist led him to give up the sport. "I was looking around to see what was next, what was available, and I suddenly thought, we have horses and carriages, so why don't I have a go at driving?" he told Horse & Hound magazine in the summer of 2017. With help from Crown Equerry Lieutenant Colonel Sir John Miller, the Duke used horses from the Royal Mews. "I borrowed four horses from the stables in London, took them to Norfolk and practised and thought, well, why not?"

Opposite: The Queen, accompanied by her two eldest children, chats with The Duke of Edinburgh during a pause in a polo game in Windsor Park, 1956

*Left: The Duke of Edinburgh
taking part in the World Carriage
Driving Championships Marathon
Competition at Windsor, 1980*

Between 1964 and 1986, Prince Philip was president
of the International Federation for Equestrian Sports
(the Swiss-based Fédération Equestre Internationale, or
FEI), and he became instrumental in helping to standardise
the international rules for carriage driving (before this,
each country had separate competition rules and events).
He also ensured that carriage driving was firmly attached
to the Royal Windsor Horse Show, and started to take part
in the event himself. In 1973, in what was only his second
driving competition, he took part in the European
Championships at Windsor, where he had to retire
with a bent axle in the last hazard of the marathon.

He went on to represent Britain in three European
Championships and six World Championships. In the 1982
World Championships in the Netherlands, the 61-year-old
Philip finished a thoroughly respectable sixth out of 39
entries, and in the same year he was the overall winner at
Windsor. "I didn't have a favourite phase," he says. "You just
had to get through them. They were all fun. It so happened
that I always did rather well at dressage, but I never managed
at the obstacles very well."

It was The Duke of Edinburgh who said that "horses are
great levellers" and he and The Queen have always taken the
vicissitudes of competition and ownership with equanimity,
delighted by their own success, but equally pleased for
others. Their tangible pleasure has, in turn, given great
pleasure to everyone else.

*Right: The Royal couple arrive with
the Royal Procession on day two of
Royal Ascot, 2016*

The country couple

As ardent advocates of the countryside, The Queen and The Duke of Edinburgh have travelled the length and breadth of Britain, savouring its wealth of natural treasures

THE FAMILIAR SIGHT of The Queen and Prince Philip in walking boots, sporting a headscarf or walking stick, respectively, is testament to the Royal couple's enduring love of the great British outdoors. The Queen's heart is in the country, which she loves for its horses, dogs and hikes through the heather, and Prince Philip's championing of the environment is matched by his passion for riding, sailing, shooting and fishing.

These are typically British tastes; and it goes without saying that the Royal couple stand for the very best in British life, including the traditions for which this country is famous around the world. News organisations love the Braemar Gathering – the annual highland games, at which Her Majesty is a chieftain – which The Queen and Prince Philip enjoy thoroughly, alongside their family.

The presence of Her Majesty or The Duke of Edinburgh at a ceremonial is a guarantee that it will be of the finest, but ceremony and long tradition are not confined to the Armed Forces. Both are proudly on display during Swan Upping, the annual swan census on the upper Thames. Nothing caveats the smartness of the turn out, the beauty of the swans, the skill of the oarsmen, the peace of the river and the good humour of all concerned – even when Swan Uppers have to dive in after swans or cygnets.

This uniquely, perhaps eccentrically, British activity helps to conserve the swan population at a time when human behaviour of other kinds is doing it no favours. Everyone involved is conscious that the very best is expected of them – and they live up to it.

Yet some of the experiences from which the Royal couple have derived most pleasure can be quite informal. The Queen and The Duke of Edinburgh have explored the whole varied landscape of the UK, besides their global adventures. Only last year, The Queen surprised Norfolk commuters by sharing their train, and delighted a couple when she and Prince Philip looked in on their wedding in Manchester. This follows in the tradition of the unintended visit that Her Majesty paid to the Cross Hands Hotel at Old Sodbury, 10 miles from The Princess Royal's home at Gatcombe, when she, two chauffeurs, two detectives, a staff member and a lady-in-waiting found themselves irretrievably trapped by a snowdrift. "It was an unbelievable honour to have her at the hotel," said the manager, Roberto Cadei. "The Queen was a lovely person."

Where do the tireless Royal couple go to relax? Until 1997, one answer might have been HMY Britannia, now in dignified retirement at Leith, providing visitors with an insight into the

Previous pages and opposite: The Queen and Prince Philip take a walk in Balmoral Castle's 7,000-hectare estate, 1972

*Right: Prince Charles, The Queen,
The Duke of Edinburgh and Princess
Anne pet two newborn Highland
calves, 1959*

"Her Majesty's private hours are spent pursuing the life of a country lady"

little-gilded simplicity of the royal's domestic taste; its chintz sofas and quilted eiderdown suggest a comfortable holiday home on the waves. More recently, they have taken their family on cruises around the Scottish coastline on MV Hebridean Princess, with picnics served on the white sands of some of the remoter islands.

On land, Her Majesty's private hours are spent pursuing the life of a country lady at Windsor, Sandringham and Balmoral, a taste inherited from her parents with whom she went deer stalking and fishing. There are smaller houses at both Sandringham and Balmoral to which she and Prince Philip can retreat for a few days before guests arrive.

Hand in hand with The Duke of Edinburgh's love of the countryside is his interest in environmental politics. Since visiting Antarctica and the South Atlantic on Britannia in late 1956 and early 1957 – as part of the Commonwealth Trans-Antarctic Expedition – Prince Philip has devoted much of his time to raising public awareness of the delicate relationship between humanity and the environment. In 1961 he was one of the co-founders of the World Wildlife Fund (now the World Wide Fund for Nature), the world's largest conservation organisation. Concern about carbon dioxide emissions led him to become one of the first citizens to use a fully electric car in the 1960s, and in recent decades has driven a eco-friendly hybrid Metrocar black cab around London.

Opposite: The Royal couple have always relished the simple pleasures of the British countryside

Opposite: The Duke of Edinburgh and The Queen enjoy themselves at the Braemer Gathering in 2015

The Duke is also a keen sportsman and, as well as enjoying polo, carriage driving and trout fishing, he has gravitated towards sailing as a hobby, as is natural for someone who served in the Royal Navy for so many years. He has long enjoyed yachting with his family and would always bring his 63-foot racing yacht, Bloodhound, on the Royal Yacht Britannia for the annual family summer holiday.

Since 1933, when the first Pembroke corgi arrived at their London home, 145 Piccadilly, in the shape of Rozavel Golden Eagle – renamed Dookie (a contraction of "Duke of York") – animals have been central to the Royal couple's private life. Many other animal species have come over the years, including – although heads of state are firmly discouraged from presenting exotic creatures as gifts – a crocodile, which The Queen could not refuse, in West Africa. It travelled to its new home in a bathtub on Britannia. Ever since 1886, when King Leopold II of the Belgians gave some racing pigeons to the Royal Family, there has been a pigeon loft at Sandringham. This still homes 160 mature birds, which race during the summer.

But it is another department at Sandringham – the Royal kennels – with which The Queen has been most closely associated,

not that she is content to simply take a few Labradors on country walks. The Labradors and spaniels at Sandringham are working dogs, trained, in former days, by The Queen herself, with help from her long-serving dog handler Bill Meldrum.

Having trained the dogs herself, The Queen personally entered gundog trials, being able to control her favourite black Labrador, Sherry, from a distance of 800 yards. Standing in front of the judges is one of the few occasions on which The Queen has confessed to nerves: the judges are blind to everything except the quality of the dog and the expertise of the handler. Not that she enters incognito: it wouldn't be much help if she did, given the dogs' names. Champions have included Sandringham Salt, Sandringham Ranger, Sandringham Slipper and Sandringham Sydney, born when Her Majesty was away in Australia.

Although The Queen no longer competes personally in field trials, she still works her dogs, picking up birds on family shooting days. And, despite having retired from public engagements, a kilted Prince Philip can still be seen alongside Her Majesty, revelling in the outdoor pursuits of the Braemar Gathering. Both quintessentially British ways to while away the day.

"The main lesson we have learnt is that tolerance is the one essential ingredient in any happy marriage. You can take it from me that The Queen has the quality of tolerance in abundance"

Prince Philip on Queen Elizabeth

The Royal Family

For kith and kin

In addition to fulfilling a hectic schedule of official duties, The Queen and Prince Philip have managed to raise their three sons and one daughter in the glare of worldwide publicity

ON 14 NOVEMBER 1948, broadcaster John Snagge read out a late-night BBC news bulletin from Buckingham Palace. He said palace officials had confirmed Princess Elizabeth, "was safely delivered of a prince". The national anthem was then played to honour the baby born to be king. Just six days before Princess Elizabeth and Prince Philip's first wedding anniversary, their first child Charles had been born.

New father Philip had been playing squash at the time with his close friend Mike Parker. He dashed back to the palace, collecting champagne and carnations on route. A huge crowd had gathered at the palace gates and even the water fountains in Trafalgar Square were dyed blue to mark the new arrival.

Within weeks, the new parents moved out of their Buckingham Palace apartment, relocating a few hundred yards down The Mall to the newly refurbished Clarence House. Two nannies, Helen Lightbody and Mabel Anderson, were hired and took charge of the royal nursery. In addition, the baby prince was watched over round the clock by armed Scotland Yard police officers, as he would be for his entire life.

By now the burden of public duty had robbed the young princess of time she would have loved to spend with her son. The King knew his beloved "Lilibet" would not only have to perform the many public engagements that he was not up to, but also had to prepare herself for the daunting role as monarch. He knew he was dying.

Philip was posted to Malta and Elizabeth decided to divide her time between her husband and her baby back home in Clarence House. Promoted to Lieutenant Commander, her husband was given command of the frigate HMS Magpie the following September. It was a period that he described as among the happiest days of his sailor life, as well as being the closest he and his wife came to living an ordinary married life. They entertained themselves with picnics

Previous pages: The Royal Family relax in a drawing room at Sandringham House, 1969

Opposite: Elizabeth with the five-week-old Prince Charles, 1948

"*The water fountains in Trafalgar Square were dyed blue to mark the new arrival*"

Opposite: The Queen and The Duke of Edinburgh with Princess Anne and Prince Charles at Balmoral Castle, 1952

and swimming expeditions, and Elizabeth behaved just like any other young officer's wife – shopping, going for coffee mornings and visiting the hairdresser.

When she was six months pregnant with her second child, Elizabeth returned to Britain for good. Princess Anne was born in August 1950. However, once again royal duty soon intervened, preventing Elizabeth from carrying out her maternal responsibilities. In the autumn of 1951, the King's rapidly declining health meant that Elizabeth and Philip had to step up and replace her parents on a royal tour of Canada and the USA.

Their next royal visit, in early 1952, was a post-war thank you to Australia and New Zealand via East Africa. A frail George VI insisted on waving his daughter and son-in-law off from the airport. The crowd gave the King a sympathetic cheer as he stood in the bitter cold to wave goodbye as his beloved daughter left for Africa. He responded to his loyal supporters with a customary wave of acknowledgement. He then turned and told Margaret "Bobo" MacDonald, Elizabeth's loyal assistant, "Look after the princess for me." She later admitted that she had never seen him so upset.

Six days later, in the early hours of 6 February 1952, George VI died of thrombosis in his sleep at Sandringham. It fell to Prince Philip, thousands of miles away in Kenya, to tell his wife that her father was dead and she was now queen. They both knew what lay ahead was a lifetime of duty; an extremely testing work schedule that would mean the time they could devote to their little children would be

Left: The Queen, Prince Philip and their children gather to celebrate the Royal couple's Silver Wedding Anniversary, 1972

"The Duke's love of country sports and outdoor life has rubbed off on all of his children"

inevitably limited. A world tour without their children was to follow, during which Charles grew ever closer to his beloved grandmother, the Queen Mother.

After months of preparation, Queen Elizabeth II was crowned in Westminster Abbey on 2 June 1953. Charles, now 4, attended the spectacular event and afterwards the young prince was brought out onto the palace balcony as Her Majesty acknowledged the cheers of the vast crowd below.

Charles, who later developed a self-deprecating sense of humour when speaking in public, was a shy little boy who stayed quietly in the background. In contrast, his boisterous younger sister delighted Philip with her boldness. Philip's intention to "toughen up" his son had the opposite effect and made the retiring Charles even more awkward and self-conscious. Indeed, it put a strain on the relationship between father and son. Some of Philip's plans, however, did work. The Duke's love of country sports and outdoor life, for instance, have rubbed off on all of his children.

The differences between Philip and Charles emerged in Jonathan Dimbleby's semi-official biography in 1994. The author portrayed Philip's parenting style as forthright

Opposite: Prince Andrew pilots a Royal Air Force helicopter in 1982

*Opposite: Princess Anne competes
at the European Three-Day Event
Championship at Burghley, 1971*

and almost bullying. There was even the suggestion that Charles felt pressured into marriage to Diana by his father. These claims were given more credibility due to the access Dimbleby had been given, which hurt Philip.

In 2001, those close to the Duke got their chance to redress the balance, saying the Duke felt his son was, "precious, extravagant and lacking in the dedication and discipline he will need if he is to make a good king." Princess Anne, too, has defended her father's parenting skills publicly, saying he is much warmer than his public persona might suggest. She described him as a loving father who read her bedtime stories and played "chasing games" with her. "Bedtime stories are things children probably don't get so much nowadays but were very important in my day," she said. The poem Hiawatha was a favourite of his.

The Royal Family grew again in 1960 with the addition of a third child, Prince Andrew. He was the first royal baby born to a reigning monarch since the birth of Queen Victoria's youngest child, Princess Beatrice, in 1857. Andrew's birth also saw the resolution of one bone of contention between The Queen and her husband, when she signed off on a change to the Royal Family's surname.

Philip had earlier complained, "I'm the only man in the country not allowed to give his name to his children." Her Majesty relented and decreed from that moment the

Left: The Queen and The Duke of Edinburgh present Prince Charles after his investiture as the Prince of Wales at Caernarvon Castle, 1969

Prince Edward marries Sophie Rhys-Jones at St George's Chapel, Windsor Castle, 1999

"The relationship between Philip and Charles has become closer in later life"

family name should be changed to Mountbatten-Windsor. Andrew's brother Prince Edward was born four years later in March, and their family was complete.

The breakdown of Charles's marriage to Princess Diana did not help relations between father and son. Philip, an outsider like the princess, tried to support his daughter-in-law, writing loving letters offering advice. Diana replied: "Dearest Pa, I was particularly touched by your most recent letter which proved to me, if I didn't already know it, that you really do care … this latest letter of yours showed great understanding and tact and I hope to be able to draw on your advice in the months ahead."

There is no doubt, however, that the relationship between Philip and Charles has become closer in later life. Charles has repeatedly praised his father in public. During the Diamond Jubilee celebrations in 2012, Philip's admission to hospital meant that he was forced to miss key weekend festivities. Charles roused the crowd with a speech in praise of Her Majesty – but also his father. "The only sad thing is my father couldn't be here," he said. "But if we shout loud enough, he might just hear us." The audience started chanting "Philip! Philip! Philip!"

A *flourishing* dynasty

After 70 years of marriage, The Queen and The Duke of Edinburgh are grandparents and great-grandparents several times over, heading up a Royal Family that is positively thriving

ON THE QUEEN'S historic 90th birthday in April 2016, Her Majesty agreed to celebrity American photographer Annie Leibovitz taking her portrait, surrounded by her five great-grandchildren and her two youngest grandchildren. She is pictured holding her youngest great-grandchild, Princess Charlotte, in her arms. Also in the touching image is her direct heir Prince George, then just two.

Zara Tindall's daughter Mia, also two, is seen proudly holding The Queen's famous black handbag, and Peter Phillips's daughters Savannah, five, and three-year-old Isla also feature prominently in the photograph taken in the Green Drawing Room, part of the Windsor Castle's semi-State apartments.

It was a special moment for The Queen, known as "Gan Gan" to George, Charlotte and her other great-grandchildren, who was also joined by the two youngest of her eight grandchildren – the Earl and Countess of Wessex's children James, Viscount Severn, aged eight, and Lady Louise Windsor. Lady Louise, then aged 12, towered above her younger relatives.

The photograph has a special place in the heart of mother of four Elizabeth II, who has welcomed the births of eight grandchildren since the arrival of Princess Anne's son Peter Phillips in June 1977. His daughter, Savannah, now six (born in 2010), was the first of five great-grandchildren. She was followed by her sister, Isla, now five, then The Queen's direct heir Prince George, now four, then Mia Tindall, now three, and finally Princess Charlotte, now two. Prince William and the Duchess of Cambridge are expecting their third child – The Queen and Prince Philip's sixth great-grandchild – early next year.

The Queen and Philip are immensely proud of their extended family. In November 1997, marking his golden wedding anniversary at London's Guildhall, the Duke spoke of his family with pride. "Like all families we went through the full range of the pleasures and tribulations of bringing up children. I am naturally somewhat biased but I think our children have done rather well under very difficult and demanding circumstances, and I hope we can be forgiven for feeling proud of them. I am also encouraged to see what a good start the next generation is making."

That "next generation" adores him too. Prince Harry, in an interview to mark The

Previous pages: The Duchess of Cambridge, Princess Charlotte, Prince George, the Duke of Cambridge, Prince Harry and The Queen during Trooping the Colour, 2016

Opposite: Zara Tindall waves to the crowd after winning team silver at the 2012 London Olympics

"Our children have done rather well under very difficult circumstances"

Queen's Diamond Jubilee in 2012, paid tribute to his grandmother's stoicism and sense of duty, but said none of her achievements would have been possible without the unswerving support of his grandfather: "I don't think that she could do it without him, especially when they're both at this age."

And Prince William, who spends as much time as possible with The Queen, learning about his future role, added, "When The Queen says well done, it means so much." William says that his relationship with his grandmother is very strong. She is always, he says, keen for him to ask questions – and he says there's nothing she won't already know, nor have a better opinion about. Indeed, it is amusing to watch them together – William towers over his grandmother and you could certainly see the pride in her eyes when she went to William's base at RAF Valley, shortly before his wedding. He was delighted to show her his helicopter.

Of course, it must be strange to have to bow or curtsey to your grandmother – but all eight of The Queen's grandchildren have been brought up to respect the institution she embodies, as well as to love their granny. They all show her the respect her rank warrants with a bow or a curtsey on their first meeting of the day.

The Royal Couple are important figures as grandparents in all their lives, from the eldest – Peter Phillips – to the youngest – James, Viscount Severn – as well as for the next generation, and they enjoy seeing them at traditional family gatherings at Easter and Christmas. The Queen is immensely proud of all her grandchildren, especially Zara Tindall, who shares her love of horses. The latter is an Eventing World Champion, was named BBC Sports Personality of the Year and won silver in the 2012 London Olympics. She was also appointed an MBE for services to equestrianism.

Not long ago, at the age of 85, The Queen was pictured on horseback looking thoroughly relaxed and content with her two youngest grandchildren, Lady Louise Windsor and her brother James. All three were enjoying a gentle ride. Lady Louise has also followed her grandfather's passion for carriage driving.

Opposite: Prince William escorts The Queen during a visit to RAF Valley, 2011

Previous pages: The Royal Family stand on the balcony at Buckingham Palace, 2017

Opposite: Prince Harry hugs his brother, Prince William, during the Invictus Games, 2014

She finds her older grandchildren useful too when trying to keep up with modern technology. The Queen has reported how they help her with her computer – but she disapproves of them spending too much time on their phones. With Prince Harry's help, she became a global viral sensation in April 2016 when she took part in a jokey video clip with her grandson and the Obamas to promote the Invictus Games.

Last year, George appeared on his first stamp after a secret photo-shoot captured The Queen and her three direct heirs to commemorate Her Majesty's 90th birthday. The picture shows the then two-year-old future king standing on blocks to make him the right height for the photograph. And, while George's parents often describe him as "naughty", Ranald Mackechnie, the photographer who took the picture, said he was a delight.

It was the second time that The Queen had agreed to an historic photo with her three direct heirs. After Prince George's christening in the Chapel Royal in St James's Palace in Oct 2013, Her Majesty proudly sat with her son Charles, grandson William and great-grandson George in the first photo of the monarch with three generations of future kings in 119 years.

The Queen, then 87, clearly relished the historic moment as she smiled broadly for the shot. The last time such a royal family portrait was taken was in 1894, when Queen Victoria was pictured with her son, later Edward VII, her grandson, crowned as George V, and her great-grandson, who became Edward VIII.

Her Majesty may be the queen of 16 realms but this is not her greatest responsibility. The most important role for Queen Elizabeth II is to be a matriarch. The head of the house of Windsor is the most senior position in the ultimate family business – one that has been passed down through generations, dynasties and centuries.

"I am privileged to witness the private side of The Queen, as a grandmother and great-grandmother. The Queen's kindness and sense of humour, her innate sense of calm and perspective, and her love of family are all attributes I experience first-hand"

Prince William on Queen Elizabeth

70 years
& counting

Post-war reconstruction

1947–1963

As the world recovered from the scars of the Second World War, The Queen and The Duke of Edinburgh witnessed a changing Britain that strove to engage with a new world order

1947

- Fashion designer Christian Dior launches "the New Look" for his summer collection. These groundbreaking designs are welcomed as a break from postwar austerity and embraced by stylish women including Princess Margaret.
- India and Pakistan gain independence from the UK on 14 August. This starts the process of partition and the displacement of some 12 million people.
- President Truman signs an act granting $400 million to fight the spread of communism, marking the start of the Cold War. Later this year, Truman creates the CIA, the Department of Defense, the Joint Chiefs of Staff and the National Security Council.

1948

- British Railways is created on 1 January as the government nationalises the railway industry. It is renamed British Rail in 1965.
- The Empire Windrush arrives in Britain on 22 June with 500 immigrants from Jamaica.
- The National Health Service launches on 5 July, giving British people the right to universal healthcare, free at the point of use.
- US-born British poet TS Eliot is awarded the Nobel Prize for Literature.
- London hosts its second Olympic Games in August. These "austerity games" are the first Olympics after a 12-year wartime hiatus.

1949

- Britain is one of 12 nations from Europe and North America to sign the North Atlantic Treaty in Washington DC, creating NATO.
- Mao Zedong's communists take control of China after a four-year civil war.
- George Orwell's dystopian novel Nineteen Eighty-Four is published in London.
- After 200,000 flights from the RAF, the USAF and other Allied air forces, the Berlin Airlift comes to an end when the Soviet Union ends its blockade of the German city.

1950

- The Archers is first broadcast on BBC Radio. The series is still running, 67 years later.
- North Korean forces, backed by China, invade South Korea, backed by the United States. The Korean War continues until 1953 when the peninsular is divided at the 38th parallel.
- Apartheid is officially launched in South Africa with the Group Areas Act.
- Comic strip Peanuts by Charles M Schulz is first published in seven US newspapers.

1951

- Jackie Brenston joins Ike Turner's Kings of Rhythm to record "Rocket 88" at Sun Studios in Memphis. With a distorted guitar sound caused by a damaged loudspeaker, it is regarded as the first ever "rock 'n' roll" single.

Previous pages: Mark I Mini cars on the assembly line, circa 1960

Opposite: The Olympic torch is presented at the 1948 Summer Olympics in London

THE IMPORTANT THING IN THE OLYMPIC GAMES IS NOT WINNING BUT TAKING PART. THE ESSENTIAL THING IN LIFE IS NOT CONQUERING BUT FIGHTING WELL.

BARON de COUBERTIN

- Winston Churchill becomes Prime Minister for the second time as the Conservative Party wins the General Election, despite receiving a quarter of a million less votes than the incumbent Labour Party.
- The Festival of Britain is launched in London. As well as opening the Royal Festival Hall, it pioneered a fresh style of architecture and design, and launched a series of arts, film and theatre exhibitions across the UK.

1952

- The first British atomic bomb is detonated off the coast of north-west Australia, making Britain the third country in the world to employ the weapon.
- Computer scientist Alan Turing, who was instrumental in cracking Nazi codes during the Second World War, is convicted of "gross indecency" after admitting to a consensual homosexual relationship. He undergoes chemical castration and commits suicide in 1954.

1953

- The blonde bombshell Marilyn Monroe arrives on the big screen in the film Niagara.
- New Zealand mountaineer Edmund Hillary and Nepalese Sherpa guide Tenzing Norgay reach the summit of Mount Everest, the highest point on earth at 29,029 ft.

- The FA Cup final is televised for the first time: 38-year-old winger Stanley Matthews excels and Stan Mortensen scores a hat-trick as Blackpool beat Bolton 4-3.
- The Twentieth-Century Fox Film Corporation announces plans to convert its entire movie-making operation to the widescreen system, Cinemascope. This begins with the biblical epic The Robe.

1954

- Dylan Thomas's "play for voices" Under Milk Wood is broadcast on BBC radio, two months after the author's death.
- Roger Bannister, a 25-year-old medical student, becomes the first man to run a mile in under four minutes, recording a time of 3 minutes and 59.4 seconds at Oxford University's Iffley Road track.
- Housewives ceremoniously tear up their ration books in Trafalgar Square as the government finally announces the end of all rationing, nine years after the end of the Second World War.
- The first two volumes of JRR Tolkien's The Lord Of The Rings – The Fellowship of the Ring and The Two Towers – are published.

1955

- The British, French and American sectors of Germany are united as West Germany and integrated into NATO. The Soviet Union responds on 1 May by forming the Warsaw Pact with its satellite states Albania, Bulgaria, Czechoslovakia, Hungary, Poland, Romania and East Germany.

- ITV launches in London on 31 October, ending the 18-year monopoly of the BBC.
- American virologist Dr Jonas Salk promotes the polio vaccine in Britain. The 500,000th person receives the vaccine.
- The latest film gimmick, 3D, is unveiled, with cinema-goers wearing red and green glasses.
- Walt Disney sees his dream of a real "Never-Never Land" come to life as Disneyland opens outside Los Angeles.
- James Dean is killed in a car crash a few months before his hit film Rebel Without A Cause is released.

1956

- Premium Savings Bonds are officially launched by Chancellor of the Exchequer Harold Macmillan in his 1956 budget.
- Egyptian leader Nasser nationalises the Suez canal in July, prompting British and French forces to seize two key ports in the Canal Zone. The ensuing Suez Crisis dominates British politics throughout the year.
- The first Routemaster bus starts public service in London, on route number 2.
- Showings of the film Rock Around The Clock, featuring Bill Haley, cause riots in cinemas across the country. Police are called to many to eject youths jiving in the aisles.

1957

- The Treaty of Rome creates the European Common Market between six countries – France, West Germany, Italy, Belgium, Holland and Luxembourg. It is aimed at the free movement of people, goods and money among the member states.
- The Soviet Union inaugurates the "space age" by putting the first artificial satellite, Sputnik 1, into orbit. A month later, the Soviets go one better when they launch a dog called Laika into space.

1958

- Prince Philip is credited with ending the tradition of the daughters of the aristocracy being presented to The Queen. Buckingham Palace does not confirm or deny this, but says the practice is not suitable for the new Elizabethan age.
- A new pressure group forms, called the Campaign for Nuclear Disarmament (CND). It calls for Britain to abandon nuclear weapons.
- A new phrase is coined by record buffs: "High Fidelity". It refers to the latest advances in stereophonic recording on disc and tape.

1959

- Duty free is launched for the first time – passengers flying overseas can now buy wine and spirits without paying any tax on them.
- Jazz continues its evolution, with several landmark albums: Giant Steps by John

Previous pages: The Festival of Britain site on the South Bank, London, 1951

Opposite: A smiling Sherpa Tenzing (left) and Edmund Hillary at their camp, having conquered Mount Everest, 1953

Coltrane, Time Out by Dave Brubeck, The Shape Of Jazz To Come by Ornette Coleman, Ah Um by Charles Mingus and Kind Of Blue by Miles Davis. The last one becomes the biggest selling jazz album of all time.
- The British Motoring Corporation (BMC) unveils its new car, the Mini.
- The M1 motorway also opens.

1960

- In April, the Quarrymen – John Lennon, Paul McCartney and George Harrison – regroup with Pete Best on drums and John's art-school friend Stuart Sutcliffe on bass. They name themselves Long John and the Silver Beatles. The first parts of the name are eventually dropped and The Beatles – with new drummer Ringo Starr – go on to dominate pop music like no other band before or since.
- After Penguin Books successfully defends against charges of obscenity, DH Lawrence's novel Lady Chatterley's Lover is published in the UK for the first time since being banned in 1928. It sells 200,000 copies in a single day.
- Plans are unveiled to construct a barrier across the Thames to shut out freak surges of water from the North Sea and protect London from tidal flooding. The resulting Thames Flood Barrier would finally be opened by Her Majesty The Queen in 1984.
- The last National Servicemen receive their call-up cards. Some 5.3 million individuals had served in the military since conscription was reintroduced in 1939.

Opposite: American trumpeter Miles Davis, whose landmark 1959 album Kind Of Blue remains the biggest-selling jazz album of all time

- John F Kennedy defeats his Republican rival Richard Nixon to become the 35th US President.

1961

- An oral contraceptive pill for women goes on the market for the first time.
- The Shakespeare Memorial Theatre in Stratford-upon-Avon is renamed the Royal Shakespeare Theatre. It houses the newly launched Royal Shakespeare Company under the aegis of artistic director Peter Hall.
- Bob Dylan makes his New York debut, much to the excitement of the audience and critics alike.

1962

- Chris Bonington and Ian Clough became the first Britons to conquer the north face of the Eiger.
- James Bond makes his big screen debut in Dr No, starring Sean Connery in the title role.
- British molecular biologists Francis Crick and Maurice Wilkins, along with American James D Watson, win the Nobel Prize in Medicine.
- Rebuilt after wartime bombing as a landmark in modernism, Coventry Cathedral is consecrated on 25 May, with a performance of Benjamin Britten's War Requiem.

1963

- President John F Kennedy is shot dead during a 10-mile presidential motorcade through Dallas on 22 November.
- The Beatles record their first LP Please Please Me, and make their national TV debut on Thank Your Lucky Stars. Beatlemania takes a firm hold in Britain later this year.
- The Great Train Robbers escape with more than £1 million. Most of the participants were later captured and jailed, although some – most notably Ronnie Biggs – escape.

Left: Paul, George, Ringo and John,
aka The Beatles, transformed the
musical landscape, 1963

A social revolution

1964–1989

Tremendous social changes were ushered in over a period that began with the sexual liberation of the 1960s and ended with the tearing down of the Berlin Wall

Bobby Moore lifts the Jules Rimet Trophy following England's victory in the World Cup final at Wembley Stadium; a game attended by The Queen and Prince Philip, 1966

Previous pages: Buzz Aldrin walks on the Moon during the Apollo 11 mission, 1969

1964

- Nelson Mandela, the leader of the African National Congress, is sentenced to life imprisonment for planning acts of sabotage against the South African state. He is sent to Robben Island, four miles west of Cape Town, sparking international protests.

1965

- Former British prime minister Sir Winston Churchill dies. Often described as "the greatest living Englishman", he achieved a world reputation not only as an all-seeing strategist and inspiring war leader, but also as a classic orator, a stylish writer, a painter of no little talent and as the shrewdest of political tacticians.
- All cigarette advertising is banned from British television.

1966

- England's football team defeats West Germany to win the World Cup on 30 July, with Geoff Hurst completing a hattrick.
- Harold Wilson's Labour party wins a second election with an increased majority.
- The government introduces random breath tests and sets an alcohol limit for drivers.

1967

- Rolling Stones frontman Mick Jagger is found guilty of having illegal substances in his possession. He is fined £100 and given a three-month prison sentence, which is later quashed.
- The "Summer of Love" sees the hippie counterculture going mainstream, first in San Francisco and then in many of the cities of North America and Europe. The movement found expression through numerous music festivals, including the Monterey Pop Festival in California and the UK's Festival of the Flower Children.

1968

- While celebrating his victory in the California Democratic presidential primary in Los Angeles, Senator Robert ("Bobby") Kennedy, the New York Senator and brother of assassinated US president John F Kennedy, is shot in the head. He dies the following day.
- Martin Luther King is shot dead in Memphis where he was leading a dustmen's strike. Within hours of his death, there are dozens of riots in major towns and cities across the US.
- A violent anti-Vietnam demo takes place in Grosvenor Square, London. The protesters try to storm the US Embassy, and 300 are arrested in the worst scenes of violence seen in the capital in years.

1969

- US astronaut Neil Armstrong speaks the following words to millions listening at home: "That's one small step for man, one giant leap for mankind." A moment later, he steps off the lunar module Eagle, becoming the first human to walk on the surface of the Moon.
- The Anglo-French supersonic airliner Concorde makes its maiden flight.

1970

- A new era in air travel is launched as the first giant jet airliner, known as the "Jumbo jet", arrives at Heathrow airport. It weighs 350 tons and carries 362 passengers – twice as many as the existing Boeing 707.
- *Monty Python's Flying Circus* becomes a cult favourite on BBC television.

1971

- Legendary designer Gabrielle "Coco" Chanel dies aged 87. She almost single-handedly revolutionised the way women looked in the 1920s, freeing them from corsets and putting them into simple yet elegant styles.
- The House of Commons votes for the UK to join the European Economic Community.
- After a great deal of opposition and discussion, the UK changes from pounds, shillings and pence to a decimal system. This takes place on 15 February, also known as "Decimalisation Day".

1972

- Eleven Israeli athletes at the Munich Olympic Games are taken hostage by Arab guerrillas. They are killed in a shoot-out between the terrorists and West German security forces.
- In the US, burglars are caught in the Democratic National Committee's offices in the Watergate complex in Washington DC. Police say they were trying to bug the opposition's headquarters.

- Apollo 17, the sixth and thus far final manned mission to the Moon, takes off.

1973

- Britain joins the European Community. Prime minister Ted Heath talks of exciting prospects, while Labour leader Harold Wilson says entry will be "crippling" for British business.
- At peace talks in Paris an agreement is reached to bring the Vietnam War to an end.
- Political leaders from London, Dublin and Belfast agree to set up a Council of Ireland to deal with problems common to all of Ireland. This follows months of violence, bombings and tit-for-tat killings.

1974

- The UK's first McDonald's hamburger restaurant opens in South London.
- US president Richard Nixon resigns over the Watergate Scandal.

1975

- The Altair, the world's first home computer, goes on sale.
- Margaret Thatcher defeats Edward Heath to become leader of the Conservative Party and Britain's first female leader of any political party.
- Harold Wilson's Labour government fulfil a 1974 election pledge to hold a referendum on EEC membership. On 5 June, the British public vote by a ratio of 62/38 to stay in the Common Market.

Opposite: The revolutionary French couturier Coco Chanel

Opposite: Hippies gather at Elysian Park in Los Angeles for a "love-in", 1967

1976

- Britain endures an unprecedented heatwave. From 23 June to 7 July, a period of 15 consecutive days, the temperature exceeds 32°C somewhere in the country.

1977

- Elvis Presley is found dead on the floor of his bathroom at the age of 42.
- The sci-fi movie *Star Wars* is released.

1978

- The world's first test-tube baby, Louise Joy Brown, is born in Oldham, Lancashire, to Lesley and Gilbert Brown.
- The Taito Corporation demonstrates a new kind of computer game in Tokyo – Space Invaders.

1979

- The "Winter of Discontent" takes hold in Britain. Unofficial strikes over the government's pay freeze disrupt many public services, with rubbish piles left uncollected and hospitals having to turn patients away.
- Margaret Thatcher becomes the first woman prime minister of Great Britain as the Conservatives sweep back into power with a majority of 43 seats in the House of Commons.

1980

- John Lennon, 40, is shot as he enters his luxury apartment building on Manhattan's Upper West Side in New York. He is rushed to St Luke's-Roosevelt Hospital Center, where he died shortly after arriving.
- Former actor Ronald Reagan defeats the incumbent Jimmy Carter to become the new President of the United States.

1981

- On 29 July nearly four billion people in 74 countries tune in to witness the marriage of Prince Charles to Lady Diana Spencer at St Paul's Cathedral.
- Bob Marley dies of cancer, aged 36. A devout Rastafarian, he has a statesman's funeral in his native Jamaica.

1982

- On 14 June, Argentina surrenders to Great Britain, ending the Falklands War.
- Channel 4 goes on air in the UK.

1983

- The BBC launch *Breakfast Time*, heralding the beginning of early-morning television in Britain.

East Germany's decision to open borders between East and West Berlin results in the fall of the Berlin Wall, 1989

- CD players go on sale for the first time in the UK.
- The UK's new £1 coin goes into circulation.

1984

- Britain's Torvill and Dean skate their way to an Olympic gold medal at the Winter Olympics in Sarajevo, scoring maximum points.
- The national miners' strike begins in the UK.
- The UK and China agree terms for returning Hong Kong to China on 1 July 1997.

1985

- Live Aid, devised by Bob Geldof, raises millions of pounds to help Africans starving as a result of the continent's worst drought for years. The concert comprises 16 hours of music from around the world, featuring many of the biggest stars of the day.
- German Boris Becker becomes the youngest player to win the Wimbledon Men's Singles title at just 17 years of age.
- The soap opera *EastEnders* starts on BBC1.

1986

- On 26 April, the world's worst nuclear power accident to date occurs at Chernobyl in the former Soviet Union (now Ukraine). While testing is taking place on one of the reactors at the Chernobyl nuclear power plant, 80 miles north of Kiev, numerous safety procedures are disregarded. At 1.23am, the reactor goes out of control, creating explosions and a fireball that blows off the heavy steel and concrete lid.

1987

- The ferry Herald of Free Enterprise capsizes with her bow doors open while leaving Zeebrugge harbour – 193 of those on board are killed.
- "Black Monday" sees stock exchanges throughout the world crash.

1988

- On 21 December, Pan Am flight 103 explodes over Lockerbie, Scotland, killing all those on board and 11 people on the ground.
- GCSE exams replace GCE O levels and CSE exams in the UK.
- Some 80,000 people celebrate the 70th birthday of Nelson Mandela at a concert at Wembley Stadium. At the time, Mandela was still in prison in South Africa for his opposition to apartheid.

1989

- Sky TV is launched, although only an estimated 50,000 homes are able to receive the new channels because of a dish shortage.
- The 28-mile-long Berlin Wall, the symbolic division between the communist and the capitalist worlds, is torn down after 28 years. East Germany's communist government had announced that its citizens would be free to travel abroad from midnight, and thousands poured through as the clock struck.

Opposite: Britain's first female prime minister, Margaret Thatcher, receives a standing ovation at the Conservative Party Conference in Blackpool, 1979

The modern era

1990–2017

While the Royal couple's marriage remains a reassuring and inspiring constant, triumphs and tribulations have continued to shape the political, social and cultural landscapes

1990

- Margaret Thatcher's 11-year spell as prime minister ends. John Major, 47, takes over.
- South African president FW de Klerk lifts the 30-year ban on the African National Congress and the South African Communist Party. Nelson Mandela and other political prisoners are released from jail.
- East and West Germany are reunited.
- Under The Channel, French and English tunnel workers bore through the last few inches of chalk separating England from France.

1991

- The Gulf War begins in January and ends in weeks as Iraqi forces are ousted from Kuwait.
- Mikhail Gorbachev resigns as the last president of the Soviet Union. Russia, Belarus and Ukraine announce a Commonwealth of Independent States.
- The Yugoslav Wars begins, signalling the end of Yugoslavia as a single nation.

1992

- Bill Clinton becomes the 42nd US president.
- Anthony Hopkins stars in The Silence of the Lambs and is awarded a knighthood.

1993

- The European Union forms a single market stretching from the Arctic to the Mediterranean and from the Atlantic to the Oder.

1994

- Nelson Mandela is inaugurated as South Africa's first black president.
- The IRA announce a "complete cessation of military operations". Three loyalist terrorist groups announce a corresponding ceasefire.
- The first National Lottery is drawn.

1995

- August is the hottest in the UK since records began in 1659, with an average daily maximum temperature of 26.5°C.
- In Paris, the presidents of Bosnia, Serbia and Croatia sign the Bosnia-Herzegovina Peace Accord, ending a conflict that claimed an estimated 200,000 lives.

1996

- The European Union imposes a worldwide ban on the export of British beef due to concerns about the transmission of "mad cow disease".
- The new bank notes of the forthcoming euro currency are unveiled in Dublin.
- Football's Euro 96 tournament is held in England and won by Germany.

1997

- Labour win a landslide victory in the General Election. Aged 43, Tony Blair becomes Britain's youngest prime minister since 1812.
- On 31 August, Diana, Princess of Wales, dies as a result of a car crash in Paris.

Previous pages: Fireworks ignite over the Olympic Stadium during the Opening Ceremony for the London 2012 Olympic Games

Opposite: Nelson Mandela, pictured just days before he was voted in as South Africa's first democratically elected black president of South Africa, 1994

1998
- President Clinton admits to an improper relationship with former White House intern Monica Lewinsky.
- David Trimble and John Hume are awarded a joint Nobel Peace Prize for their work in ending the conflicts in Northern Ireland.

1999
- In August, parts of England see their first total eclipse since 1927. There won't be another in the UK until 2090.
- A minimum wage is introduced throughout the UK for the first time.

2000
- The new millennium is officially ushered in in the UK with the opening of the Millennium Dome in London.
- IT workers manage to prevent any problems caused by the Y2K bug, caused by computers using two-year date fields.

2001
- On 11 September, 19 Islamic fundamentalists hijack four planes, crashing two into the World Trade Center in New York and one into the Pentagon in Washington. The fourth comes down in a field in western Pennsylvania. Nearly 3,000 are killed in the attacks.
- Trinidad-born British writer VS Naipal is awarded the Nobel Prize for Literature.

2002
- The Commonwealth Games are held in Manchester in July and August.
- East Timor gains independence from Indonesia.

2003
- In March, the UK and the US declare war on Iraq following Saddam Hussein and his sons' refusal to leave the country.
- England win the Rugby World Cup for the first time, defeating host nation Australia in the final.

2004
- The Scottish Parliament building is formally opened by The Queen at Holyrood in Edinburgh.
- The Queen christens the largest ocean-going liner in the world, the Queen Mary II, named after her grandmother, Mary of Teck.
- A tsunami on Boxing Day causes devastation in Asia, leaving more than 230,000 people dead.

2005
- Four terrorists plant bombs on London's tubes and buses, killing 52 and injuring more than 700.
- Tony Blair wins a third successive election.
- British playwright Harold Pinter is awarded the Nobel Prize for Literature.

2006
- The 21st Bond film, Casino Royale, opens in November with actor Daniel Craig in the lead role. He is the sixth actor to play the role.

Opposite: Tony Blair, Britain's first Labour Prime Minister since 1979, with his wife Cherie on the steps of 10 Downing Street after his election victory, 1997

- The Queen opens the Senedd debating chamber of the national assembly for Wales.
- Helen Mirren wins a Best Actress Oscar for her portrayal of Her Majesty in Stephen Frears's film The Queen.

2007

- The rebuilt Wembley Stadium is completed.
- Tony Blair steps down as prime minister after 10 years and is replaced by Gordon Brown.
- British novelist Doris Lessing wins the Nobel Prize for Literature.
- The UK's terrestrial television switchover to digital begins in Whitehaven, Cumbria.

2008

- Lewis Hamilton, 23, is crowned the youngest ever Formula I champion.
- The global financial crisis deepens. The UK government nationalises Northern Rock and Wall Street bank Lehman Brothers files for bankruptcy.
- Barack Obama is elected US President, the first African American to win the presidency.

2009

- The Office for National Statistics announces that the UK economy is officially in recession for the first time since 1991.
- Harry Patch, last survivor of the First World War trenches, dies aged 111.

- The G20 summit is held in London in response to the global financial crisis.

2010

- Ash from Iceland's Eyjafjallajökull volcano triggers the closure of European airspace for six days.
- ITV holds the UK's first televised election debate between the three main party leaders. The general election resulted in a hung parliament, with David Cameron as prime minister and Nick Clegg as deputy prime minister.
- The King's Speech, a film about Her Majesty The Queen's father George VI, wins four Academy Awards.
- A group of 33 miners in Chile are rescued after 69 days trapped 2,300 ft underground.

2011

- There are riots in London and other parts of the UK after police shoot a man dead in Tottenham.
- The Government sets up the Leveson inquiry to examine the role of the media.
- The "Arab Spring" sees unrest spread through much of the Arab world, forcing leaders from power in Tunisia, Egypt, Libya and Yemen.

2012

- The Scottish government announces plans to hold a referendum on Scottish independence.

Vast crowds gather on the shores of Sydney Harbour to see in the new millennium

- Bradley Wiggins becomes the first British winner of the Tour de France in the race's 110-year history.
- London becomes the first city to host its third Summer Olympic Games. The previous occasions were in 1908 and 1948.

2013
- Sir Alex Ferguson retires as Manchester United manager after 27 years.
- Andy Murray wins the Men's Singles at Wimbledon after defeating Novak Djokovic in straight sets. He is the first British man to win the title since Fred Perry in 1936.
- The General Synod of the Church of England votes in favour of allowing the ordination of women bishops.

2014
- The first gay marriages are conducted in the UK in March.
- Scotland votes "No" to independence by a margin of 55.3 per cent to 44.7 per cent. It is the highest vote turnout – 84.5 per cent – in any UK election since universal suffrage.
- Golfer Rory McIlroy wins The Open and the PGA – his third and fourth major titles.

2015
- Scottish-born economist Angus Deaton wins the Nobel Prize for Economics.
- In the General Election on 7 May, David

Cameron wins a second term as Prime Minister, this time with an overall majority.
- London singer Adele's third album, 25, sells more than 3 million copies in a single week in the US alone. It goes on to sell more than 20 million copies internationally.

2016
- The year is marked the death of an unusually high number of much-loved celebrities, including David Bowie, Prince, George Michael, Alan Rickman, Johan Cruyff, Zaha Hadid, Muhammad Ali, Leonard Cohen, Carrie Fisher and Debbie Reynolds.
- The UK votes to leave the European Union, prompting the resignation of prime minister David Cameron, who is succeeded by Theresa May.
- Donald Trump wins the US presidency.
- Bob Dylan is awarded the Nobel Prize for Literature.

2017
- Prime minister Theresa May announces a snap General Election in June. The Conservative Party loses its overall majority, resulting in a hung Parliament.
- England beat India by nine runs to win the Women's Cricket World Cup for the fourth time.
- Japanese-born British novelist Kazuo Ishiguro wins the Nobel Prize for Literature.

Opposite: Barack Obama becomes the 44th President of the United States, having won the 2008 election by a majority of 10 million votes

Right: Andy Murray becomes the
first British male to win a Wimbledon
singles title since Fred Perry, 2013

"Time and again, quietly and modestly, The Queen has shown us all that we can confidently embrace the future without compromising the things that are important"

Prince William on Queen Elizabeth

The platinum collection

Fit for royalty

Inspired by Korea's regal past and tradition of expert craftsmanship,
Nadri produces jewellery of majestic beauty and enduring quality

THE ROYALS OF the Silla Dynasty, who ruled one of the three ancient kingdoms of Korea from 57 BC for nearly a thousand years, were buried in the finest jewellery that their artisans could produce. Their tombs were filled with intricate golden crowns, swords, rings and necklaces, earning the country's craftsmen a reputation as experts in working the precious yellow metal. They can't have known it then but, more than 2,000 years later, their treasures would steer the course of another Korean man's life, helping him build his own jewellery empire, Nadri.

The firm's founder, Young Tae MacGyver Choi, remembers an inspiring trip to the National Museum in Gyeongju, South Korea. "I was fascinated by how beautiful and detailed the jewellery was," says Young. "There was a tiny gold crown, now unearthed and displayed behind glass, that had been lovingly laboured over – it was perfect. Seeing jewellery that has stood the test of time, of such quality, shapes the way that I make Nadri jewellery today."

Young's museum visit, along with a memorable school trip to a mining factory, set the course for his career. The son of a farmer in Goseong County who milled rice for his village,

Young knew he couldn't continue his family's business as he was the youngest of six siblings. So, in the early 1980s, he joined a jewellery manufacturer where he learnt his trade.

"I eventually launched Nadri when I was confident that, if I put my time and my mind into it, I could make the very finest jewellery," he says. "My goal was to create an everlasting brand; work that could be cherished for years."

In 1997, Young moved to America to train a team and take the company global. Thirty-three years on from its founding, Nadri's products now adorn the necks, ears and fingers of women across the world.

Instead of employing a single style, the company specialises in creating pieces for a range of different tastes and occasions. Young and old, Nadri's clients come to the counters of prestigious department stores for everything from a simple cuff, dotted with cubic zirconia stones, to a statement string of pearls complete with tassels for a black-tie dinner. Customers often own several pieces, with the company's work akin to fine jewellery, but without the eye-watering price tag. "Jewellery is the final touch to

complete your look," says Young, "and women appreciate affordable luxury."

When Nadri started out it was a one-man operation, with Young doing everything from designing to manufacturing to sales. Now based in New York, Nadri draws upon a design team – all of them trained at prestigious and internationally accredited art schools – who travel to Europe and look to fashion, art, nature and vintage jewellery for inspiration. Teams source materials from around the world and send only the finest to state-of-the-art factories in Southeast Asia.

Each of Nadri's collections is connected by a golden thread – the quest for perfection. Each design is made using fine jewellery techniques, from hand-setting each cubic zirconia to hand-polishing each gemstone. Each of these techniques is a nod to those early artisans' attention to detail in 57 BC.

Young is proud of how far Nadri has come over the past three decades – from his spark of an idea as a boy in Korea to an international luxury jewellery brand. "Together," he says, "we are accomplishing the dream that was started back in 1984."
www.nadri.com

The making of a masterpiece

A symphony of striking sculptural form and unsurpassed function, the speakers engineered by Estelon are works of pure audio art

THERE CAN BE few world-class firms that have been founded at the breakfast table, but Estelon – from Tallinn, Estonia – is certainly one of them. The high-end audio brand traces its origins back to a morning in April 2010 when engineer Alfred Vassilkov was having a casual discussion with his family.

"It was a lovely Sunday morning with the entire family all having breakfast together," Alfred recalls. "I had long held the ambition of creating the world's best loudspeaker. I knew what the concept would be and, rather than sell the idea to another company, I decided to try it on my own. Luckily, I already had the best key executives in the family: my daughters Alissa and Kristiina. That very same evening, we decided to set up the business using our family savings. By Tuesday, the company was legally established."

Alfred had been designing speakers for other companies for over 25 years and spent five years researching opportunities to achieve his ambition of creating the world's best speaker. He always sought perfection and overcame challenges: growing up in the Soviet era, when resources were limited, he dismantled radios to rebuild and

improve them. He took this interest to university, studying electro-acoustics in St Petersburg.

These experiences enabled Alfred to develop technologies and find materials with which to construct unique and innovative products. These were combined with inspiration from nature – particularly from the lush and expansive forest landscapes of Estonia – to create the perfect balance between engineering and design.

The result was Estelon, one of the world's most luxurious speaker brands. It derives aesthetic and acoustic excellence through the merger of ingenious creativity and cutting-edge science. Each decision – from engineering techniques to the materials and components used in the manufacturing process – is made with the perfect harmony of the speakers as a whole in mind.

For Alfred, this flawless synergy is what an engineer strives for in his or her creations. Every single detail is carefully considered, selected and tested during all stages of the production process. The result is a handcrafted masterpiece of beauty on the outside and the pinnacle of technology on the inside.

Estelon is today regarded as a leading innovator in the audio industry, having received multiple awards for its designs and technological innovations. In 2015, the company's flagship loudspeaker, the Estelon Extreme, scooped the Best of Innovation Award in the High Performance Audio and Video category at the Consumer Electronics Show in Las Vegas. In addition, the Estelon X Diamond has been named Product of the Year by Absolute Sound Magazine, while other Estelon products have won numerous editor's choice and best performance awards around the world.

The company's loudspeakers are today proudly owned by some of the world's most eminent innovators and global leaders. Ultimately, Alfred feels that they are intended for sophisticated individuals who appreciate the finer things in life to enjoy in their homes.

"A lifetime of designing and engineering unique audio products enabled me to blend mature character into a young audio brand," says Alfred. "This has been key in ensuring that Estelon speakers are among the best in the world."

www.estelon.com

A sparkling legacy

With three decades of dazzling success behind her, jeweller Sharon Khazzam creates exquisite pieces that are destined to be treasured for generations to come

JEWELLERY DESIGNER SHARON Khazzam's studio is on a quiet, tree-lined street. But walk through the doors and it's like stepping into a Moroccan treasure trove or prising open a sunken treasure chest to reveal a spectacular horde of gems. Giant, paintbox-coloured stones sit in oyster shells on Khazzam's desk alongside piles of tiny precious gems. The walls are painted a bright orange and tacked with inspirational images, and on her drafting board are intricate work-in-progress paintings of new ideas.

The delight on discovering her eclectic studio space gives a clue as to why Khazzam has enjoyed a three-decade-long career, is honoured as a member-at-large by the American Society of Jewelry Historians and, in 2014, was inducted into the Council of Fashion Designers of America. Much like the interior of her studio, Khazzam's designs are a burst of colour that can't help but brighten the day of the women who wear them.

It took years for Khazzam to find the right source for the stones she needs, be they rare pink padparadscha sapphires or tourmalines. "The most important thing is having a relationship with your gem dealers, a friendship," she says. "Each person is strong in regions of the world or stones." Her connections with dealers were forged when she took her first job with Asprey in the 1980s and later, in 1993, when she ventured out under her own name. "Now I have a gem dealer who I know will find a stone for me, if it exists," says Khazzam. "He's extremely strong in a gem that I adore – a paraiba tourmaline. I am obsessed with it. It's very, very rare, from Brazil. It's the colour of the Caribbean waters; a deep blue that you feel you want to dive into."

Though getting to work and play with sparkling precious stones daily might be the obvious reason for Khazzam being drawn into the jewellery world, it was in fact painting that got her hooked. "It is by default that I am a jewellery designer," she explains. "I fell in love with it because, at university, you had to paint designs in miniature; that's what caught me, really. My favourite part of the process is still to sit at my drawing board and just paint."

Her approach could be considered quaint in an era of computer-assisted designs, but hand sketching affords her creations more character and expression. "It's funny," she says. "I am constantly being approached by people who keep insisting that I start working with a computer, that it's so passé to hand draw every design. But I feel that it's very important, not only to me but also to my clients. They appreciate the time it takes for me to actually draw it rather than sit at a computer and press buttons. The whole idea is to have a unique jewel. Nothing is perfect. If everything is perfect then you can duplicate the designs and I feel that loses a little bit of what I do."

Khazzam's desire to create uniqueness means that she is adventurous with the scale of her pieces – a case in point being the huge starburst she wears around her neck daily. Her stones are unusual, as are her colour combinations, and she doesn't follow any jewellery trends. There's a timelessness to her work. "I try to make pieces that will last way past my generation, my children's generation and their grandchildren," she says. With three decades of design behind her, Khazzam is well on her way.

www.sharonkhazzam.com

The natural choice

Luxury skincare brand JK7 uses only organic ingredients in its carefully curated range of exclusive, high-end products

WHEN JURGEN KLEIN, founder of skincare company Jurlique, sold his brand and moved with his wife, Karin, to Hawaii to set up a luxury spa retreat, he was determined to leave the skincare market behind him.

"He was sick and tired of the lies people tell in the industry," says Karin. "But then he started to make his own spa products in the commercial kitchen, and they were wonderful. I challenged him to stop complaining and instead to create something better than what was available commercially. I said: 'Can you bring a product to market that is truly natural, organic and high performing with no chemicals at any stage of production?' He was hesitant – he's a biochemist and knows the difficulties – but he rose to the challenge."

And so, in 2015, after seven years of research and testing, JK7 was born. It is a pure, organic and anti-ageing, high-end skincare brand, handmade in tiny batches, using only the best natural ingredients and the most precious and expensive essential oils (including rose, myrrh and jasmine), powerful JK7 Signature Extracts and healing herbs. They are designed to improve the health of the skin, as well as its appearance.

In fact, university-commissioned research found that one star ingredient in JK7's signature extract, the rind of the mangosteen fruit, has anti-cancer properties, inhibiting malignant melanoma cells from spreading. The company can't, however, put this on the label because cosmetics are not classified as medicines.

"The abundance of herbal and natural ingredients in our products creates a synergy to help the skin function exactly as it's supposed to," says Karin. "We can't stop skin ageing – any cream that claims that is lying – but we can work against free radicals, preventing protein degeneration and accelerated ageing. We see skincare as one of the tools for a better, healthier holistic lifestyle. Our customers tend to be people who already have a high awareness of ecology and of their bodies, and who make conscious choices about the products they use. Kathy Freston, best-selling vegan author, is one of our fans."

The range is currently available for purchase in London, New York, Hawaii, Switzerland and Austria, from selected spas, hotels, high-end retail outlets and airport lounges, and is about to be launched in the Netherlands and Japan. Products can also be

bought online via JK7's website. Future plans include an all-natural skin-whitening cream that works against age spots and discoloration, as well as expansion into the Far East and Australia.

There are now 22 different products in the range, including face washes, serums and lotions. Given the purity and expense of the ingredients, the products are positioned at the very top end of the market, with the best-selling Serum Lotion – a luxurious day-and-night anti-ageing serum for all skin types – costing £1,415 for a 30 ml glass bottle.

"Our skincare is very exclusive and will never be for the mass market, or available everywhere," explains Karin. "That's because we took the decision not to compromise on quality or standards at any stage of the process. For example, each plant extraction takes about 50 hours with our spagyric extraction method that enhances the lifeforce of each healing plant, and every bottle is hand-sterilised, hand-filled and hand-packed. We have created something that is truthful and effective, as well as luxurious. There is no comparison anywhere else on the market."
www.jk7skincare.com

Storied stones

Like its country of origin, India's Kohinoor Jewellers blends influences old and new to distinctive and beautiful effect

AGRA IS A city steeped in history, famous for the iconic white marble Taj Mahal built by Mughal emperor Shah Jahan. The former Mughal capital has for centuries also been home to jewellers, artisans and artists inspired by the rich heritage around them.

Family-owned and now in its fifth generation, the exclusive, appointment-only Kohinoor Jewellers creates distinctive pieces for a discerning global clientele. "Our business developed out of our heritage," says owner Ghanshyam Mathur. "Now we work with a contemporary fusion of art and jewellery based on Indian art, architecture and paintings."

The Mathur family's ancestors came to the old walled city of Agra in 1857 with the court of the last Mughal emperor Bahadur Shah Zafar. Since then, the family has collected fine gemstones, jewellery and art, becoming experts in the intricacies of Indian art over the generations. Ghanshyam, like his father before him, is a connoisseur of Indian art collected from diverse regions, periods and religions.

"We never run out of inspiration," he says. "There is so much variety in our past. And, of course, we have the Taj Mahal itself, which was the inspiration for the Taj Signature Collection." Not that all inspiration comes from distant history. "My son Milind and I play golf, so we created a very successful golf-themed collection," he says. "We also created a collection based on Bharatanatyam, a classical Indian dance, using the shapes and elegance of the dancers."

The artistry and love of colour and pattern in Kohinoor's jewellery is expressed through gemstones of the highest quality. "Our jewellery is all about the stones, sapphires from Sri Lanka, for example, and rubies from Burma," says Ghanshyam. "We tend to buy stones in rough form and cut them to our specification." Often Kohinoor's jewellery begins not with a design but with the gemstones themselves, the design serving to enhance and display their particular qualities.

Fifth-generation Ruchira Mathur is Kohinoor's designer and works alongside her brother Milind Mathur, who is a graduate gemologist, certified by the Gemological Institute of America, and the company's Artistic Director. "They both have a flair for working with gemstones," says Ghanshyam, "It's in their blood." Ruchira and Milind bring a western sensibility to the jewellery collections, attuned to the tastes of the international visitors who come to Agra.

"Our jewellery is exposed to worldwide trends," says Ghanshyam. "Our customers demand the best quality and they know their jewellery. They immediately see that we offer very fine pieces." Each collection from Kohinoor Jewellers is one of a kind.

The company also offers a bespoke jewellery service, which is particularly suited to overseas visitors staying in Agra. The combination of stones and choice of settings are discussed and detailed design options created. The finished pieces are then shipped on completion.

Kohinoor Jewellers exactly defines what Ghanshyam calls "contemporary fusion": the perfect setting of expertly cut gemstones, reflecting the cultural and artistic traditions of India, and a stylish ability to bring these strands together in refined contemporary jewellery. "This fusion of modern, bespoke and heritage comes through in all our work," says Ghanshyam. As in-the-know visitors to Kohinoor Jewellers have discovered, the Taj Mahal isn't the only thing of beauty worth seeing in Agra.

www.kohinoorjewellers.com

"For me, heaven is likely to be something of a comedown"

Queen Elizabeth

Appendices

Wedding gifts to Princess Elizabeth and The Duke of Edinburgh

Princess Elizabeth and Philip Mountbatten received more than 2,500 wedding gifts from well-wishers around the world, some of which were put on display for a few days in a charity exhibition at St James's Palace. Alongside 500 tins of pineapple, crystallised fruits, sugared almonds and numerous tins of salmon, the Royal couple received 76 handkerchiefs, 30 scarves, 148 pairs of stockings, 16 nightgowns and an electric washing machine. The staggering haul of presents also included the following…

- The people of Burma presented a necklace of 96 rubies in a gold setting, engraved with the world "Burma". It was a symbolic gift: in traditional Burmese beliefs, rubies protect their owner from evil and illness, and there are believed to be 96 diseases that can affect humans.

- The Swiss Federal Council gave a diamond-encircled watch and wristlet.

- The Australian government presented a handwoven merino wool cloak, woven by Australian war widows from 18 yards of cloth. It has an ice-blue silk lining with an Aussie motif, and hand-drawn silver buttons with an Aboriginal design.

- The Markgravine of Baden in Germany presented a diamond and ruby brooch.

- A carved rosewood necklace in a tooled leather jewel case was given by Colonel Samuel J Sutherland of the US Army.

- A Boucheron ruby necklace from the bride's parents, with earrings made with wedding gift pearls.

- A live turkey, sent by an American girl who was concerned about the food supply in postwar Europe.

- A medallion commemorating the coronation of Queen Victoria, from Miss LT Sykes.

- An uncut diamond from the people of Tanganyika. "The cutting of the stone will be arranged in accordance with the Princess Elizabeth's wishes," reads an accompanying note.

- A gold tiara, chased in openwork with symbolic devices, presented by the Emperor of Ethiopia, Haile Selassie I. It has never been worn publicly.

- A gold pen from the Chartered Institute of Secretaries.

- A carved ivory brooch in the form of a wheatsheaf and a pair of earrings, from Mrs Edgar Strange.

- A gold, diamond and enamel brooch in the form of the badge of the Guild Air Pilots, from the Marquis and Marchioness of Londonderry.

- A diamond and ruby brooch in the form of a butterfly, from the Dowager Countess of Onslow.

- Two handmade bird brooches, from the Men of the Disabled Sailors and Soldier Work

- A feather brooch in the form of a wild duck, from Miss Betty Butler.

- 24 pairs of gloves, including a pair of handmade gloves from Miss Edith Dadson.

- A diamond and platinum Cartier necklace was presented by the Nizam of Hyderabad. It was later taken apart and – along with the Burmese ruby necklace – reassembled by the jewellers Garrard in 1973. Garrard took the 96 Burmese rubies and the diamonds from the necklace to create the iconic Burmese Ruby Tiara. It presents the rubies as wreaths of roses, separated by rays of diamonds, and is believed to be the Queen's favourite tiara, one she frequently wears on State occasions.

- A pair of gold and amethyst cufflinks from the Lord and Lady Delamere.

- A refrigerator, from the Women's Voluntary Service.

- A Singer sewing machine from the Provost and Council of Clydebank.

- A snapshot album with a lid decorated in the traditional Ukrainian style, presented by a Ukrainian Prisoners of War camp in Sleaford, Lincolnshire.

- An engraved vase from President Truman and Bess Truman.

- A set of golden glass goblets from President Edvard Beneš of Czechoslovakia.

- Sevres and Meissen porcelain from the French government.

- A silver guilt dressing case from the Diplomatic Corps.

- A ruby and diamond trellis gold brooch from the Director of Garrard & Co Ltd jewellers.

- An ecru tablecloth, handworked and embroidered, from the National Federation of Women's Institutes. It also presented a hardbound volume with a page contributed by each of the 58 county organisations that comprise the federation.

- A copy of The Book of Common Prayers and Hymns Ancient & Modern, presented by an anonymous admirer.

- A Georgian silver salver with scalloped corners on scroll feet, and a cornelian and agate seal, presented by Noel Coward.

- A 19th-century diamond fringe necklace was presented as a joint present from the Lord Mayor of London and the Court of Aldermen, the Governor of the Bank of England, the Chairman of the Stock Exchange, the Chairman of Lloyds, the Chairman of the Baltic Exchange and the Committee of London Clearing Banks.

- Among the 148 pairs of stockings were a pair of nylons from Miss J Lawrence.

- Twelve bottles of sloe gin, from Mr Michael Farr.

- A diamond and turquoise shamrock brooch from the Dowager Duchess of Portland.

- A piece of crocheted cotton lace, made from yarn personally spun by Mahatma Gandhi, presented by the government of India. The central motif on the cloth reads "Jai Hind" ("Victory for India"). It received some scorn from Queen Mary, who mistook it for a loincloth. "Such an indelicate gift," she is said to have remarked. "What a horrible thing."

- A sapphire and diamond feather brooch from Messrs Carrington and Co. Ltd.

- Carved cameo in a case, from Major AE Murray.

- A diamond and ruby necklace and a string of pearls from Elizabeth's mother and father.

- A gold and jade necklace from King Farouk of Egypt.

- A writing desk from the government of New Zealand.

- Pieces from a Chinese porcelain dinner service, given by President Chiang Kai Shek of the Chinese Republic. The China was printed with characters denoting "double joy".

- The Central Council and Members of the Royal Overseas League presented a diamond, ruby and sapphire clip brooch in the form of the badge of the league.

- A picnic basket from Princess Margaret.

- A movie camera from King George VI.

- A gold lace-work brooch set with diamonds and rubies from the Jewellers and Silversmiths of Great Britain.

- A gold and jewelled brooch convertible into two clips, typical of Portuguese workmanship, presented by British subjects from various Commonwealth nations and friends of Portuguese East Africa.

- A hand-knitted cardigan.

- A silver and paste brooch from Miss P Haberman.

- A brooch set with pearl from Ross-shire Rivers from the people of Ross and Cromarty.

- An Italian cameo brooch from Miss M Hatswell.

- Two pairs of jewelled anklets, set with brilliants and enamel drops, mounted as a necklace, presented by the Dominion of India.

- An antique Rajput headpiece of gold set with pearls, rubies and diamonds, presented by the Maharao Raja Shri Bahadur Singh Bahadur of Bundi (a princely state, now part of Rajasthan, India). This headpiece, traditionally worn by the Rulers of Bundi, has now been mounted as a brooch.

- A bead necklace from Mr John Jefferys.

- A blue necklace and bracelets from Miss Neta Ferrarini.

- An oval agate brooch from Mr WF Rowe.

- Two sets of shell jewellery from Miss Alice Watson.

- As well as a book-case, Elizabeth's grandmother, Queen Mary, presented her with a tiara. Known as "Granny's tiara", it was initially a wedding present for Mary herself in 1893, designed by Garrard and commissioned by Lady Eve Greville on behalf of the Girls Of Great Britain and Ireland. Originally a diamond design of festoons and scrolls, set on a bandeau base of round and lozenge-shaped diamonds, it was modified by Mary in 1914, who removed the base and replaced the pearls with simpler diamond collets. It became one of the Queen's most commonly worn tiaras.

- An HMV radiogram from the conductor and composer Sir Malcolm Sergeant.

- A gold and cairngorm brooch from the members of His Majesty's Medical Household in Scotland.

- A diamond flower and spray brooch from the Grand Master Mason, Office Bearers and Brethren of the Grand Lodge of Scotland.

- A ruby and diamond pendant from the All Burmese Women's Freedom League.

- An agate jewel casket mounted with silver from the Earl and Countess Beauchamp.

- Three gold safety pins in a case from Mr P Stewart.

- The 16th Fifth Lancers presented a badge of the regiment in gold, enamel, rubies and diamonds.

- A diamond and sapphire pendant in the form of a star from the Lord and Lady Jessel.

- A diamond wrist watch from Mrs R Benham.

- A chased silver flower ring from the "Girl of Malaya".

- An Iona green stone from Mr Hector Maclean and the people of Iona.

- The Members of the Canadian Legion of the British Empire Service League presented a gold maple-leaf brooch set with diamonds and bearing the badge of the league in enamel and diamonds.

- A gold tie pin, mounted with a miniature of George IV, from Mrs E Stuart Clark.

- A gold chain and heart-shaped pendant with Ceylon stones from Mrs CE Albrecht.

- A gold and enamel flower brooch from the Reverend F Keeling Scott.

- A gold and enamel tie pin bearing Queen Victoria's cypher from Mrs F Hooker.

- Silver napkin ring from Girl Guide Shirley Roberts.

- A gold watch set in the form of a key from Mr Henry L Lambert.

- Three Czechoslovak jewelled brooch ornaments from Czech children of a secondary school in Prague.

- An oval gilt brooch with flower designs worked in satin by the donor, Miss Amy Douler.

- The Returned Soldiers', Sailors', and Airmen's Imperial League of Australia (RSSAILA) presented a brooch representing a spray of flowering gum in gold and black opals contained in a casket, bearing in gold the badge of the organisation.

- A gold brooch set with diamonds and rubies in a trellised floral design presented by Prince Louis II on behalf of the Principality of Monaco.

- A jewelled brooch from Miss F Grunberg.

- A heart-shaped pendant in gold filigree and enamel from Madame Maria V de Carvalho.

- A large uncut pink diamond, presented by the Canadian geologist Dr John Thorburn Williamson. This 23.6-carat stone from Tanzania is thought to be one of the rarest and finest diamonds in existence and is probably the single most valuable gift received. It was set into a flower-shaped silver brooch by Cartier in 1953 (The Queen's favourite "Williamson brooch") and is thought to be worth more than £6 million today.

- An opal and gold pendant in a gold chain from the City Council of Brisbane, Queensland, Australia.

- A pair of opal earrings from the Queensland Branch of the Royal Society of St George.

- A pear shell containing seven large pearls from the Bahraini ruler Salman Bin Hamed Alk Helifahn.

- Two engraved silver crosses from Miss Elizabeth Elin.

- A silver filigree brooch from Mrs I Woodcock.

- A cameo brooch representing Joan of Arc from Mrs O Baker.

- A brooch of New Zealand greenstone mounted with gold from Mr John Ewan.

- An unset cameo, featuring the head of King George VI, from Mr D Shapio.

- A gold and ruby tie pin from Miss EM Bratby.

- A hand-knitted tea cosy.

- A Scottish silver brooch and cuff links from the second Orkney troop boy scouts.

- Two pairs of bed socks.

The Royal Family tree

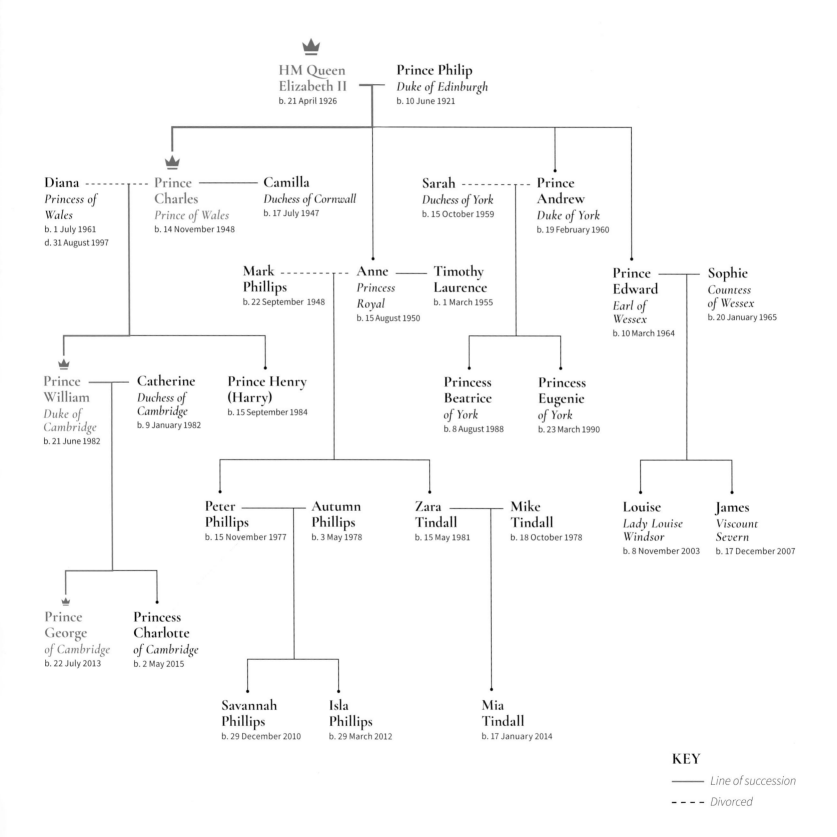

KEY

——— *Line of succession*

- - - - *Divorced*

State Visits paid by The Queen and The Duke of Edinburgh

DATE	COUNTRY	HOST
24–26 June 1955	Norway	King Haakon VII
8–10 June 1956	Sweden	King Gustaf VI
18–21 February 1957	Portugal	President Craveiro Lopes
18–21 February 1957	France	President René Coty
21–23 May 1957	Denmark	King Frederick IX
17–21 October 1957	USA	President Eisenhower
25–27 March 1958	Netherlands	Queen Juliana
26 February–1 March 1961	Nepal	King Mahendra
2–6 March 1961	Iran	Shahanshah Mohammad Reza Shah Pahlari
2–5 May 1961	Italy	President Gronchi
5 May 1961	Vatican City	Pope John XXIII
23 November 1961	Liberia	President Tubma
1–8 February 1965	Ethiopia	Emperor Haile Selassie
8–12 February 1965	Sudan	Dr El Tigani
18–23 May 1965	Germany	President Lübke
9–13 May 1966	Belgium	King Badouin and Queen Fabiola
5–11 November 1968	Brazil	President de Costa e Silva
11–18 November 1968	Chile	President Frei
5–10 May 1969	Austria	President Jonas
18–25 October 1971	Turkey	President Sunay
10–15 February 1972	Thailand	King Bhumibol and Queen Sirikit
13–14 March 1972	Maldives	President Nasir
15–19 May 1972	France	President Pompidou
17–21 October 1972	Yugoslavia	President Tito
15–22 March 1974	Indonesia	President Soeharto
24 February–1 March 1975	Mexico	President Echeverria
7–12 May 1975	Japan	Emperor Hirihito
25–28 May 1976	Finland	President Kekkonen
6–11 July 1976	USA	President Ford
8–12 November 1976	Luxembourg	Grand Duke Jean and Grand Duchess Joséphine

DATE	COUNTRY	HOST
22–26 May 1978	Germany	President Scheel
16–19 May 1979	Denmark	Queen Margrethe and Prince Henrik
27 July–1 August 1979	Zambia	President Kuanda
29 April–2 May 1980	Switzerland	President Chevallaz
14–17 October 1980	Italy	President Partini
17 October 1980	Vatican City	Pope John Paul II
21–23 October 1980	Tunisia	President Bourguiba
25–27 October 1980	Algeria	President Chadli
27–30 October 1980	Morocco	King Hassan II
5–8 May 1981	Norway	King Olav V
26 February–6 March 1983	USA	President Reagan
25–28 May 1983	Sweden	King Carl XVI Gustaf and Queen Silvia
26–30 March 1984	Jordan	King Hussein and Queen Noor
25–29 March 1985	Portugal	President and Senhora Eanes
17–21 February 1986	Nepal	King Birendra and Queen Aishwarya
12–18 October 1986	China	President Li Xiannian
17–21 October 1988	Spain	King Juan Carlos and Queen Sofia
25–27 June 1990	Iceland	President Vigdis Finnbogadottir
14–16 May 1991	USA	President Bush
9–12 June 1992	France	President Mitterand
19–23 October 1992	Germany	President Von Weizsacker
4–7 May 1993	Hungary	President Goncz
17–20 October 1994	Russia	President Yeltsin
25–27 March 1996	Poland	President Walesa
27–29 March 1996	Czech Republic	President Havel
28 October–1 November 1996	Thailand	King Bhumibol
19–22 April 1999	South Korea	President Kim Dae-jung

DATE	COUNTRY	HOST	DATE	COUNTRY	HOST
16–19 October 2000	Italy	President Ciampi	13–16 May 2008	Turkey	President Gul
30 May–1 June 2001	Norway	King Harald V & Queen Sonja	21–22 October 2008	Slovenia	President Turk
5–7 April 2004	France	President Jacques Chirac	23–24 October 2008	Slovakia	President Gasparovic
2–4 November 2004	Germany	President Horst Kohler	24–25 November 2010	UAE	Emir Khalifa
16–17 October 2006	Lithuania	President Adamkus	25–28 November 2010	Oman	Sultan Qaboos
18–19 October 2006	Latvia	President Vike-Freiberga	17–20 May 2011	Ireland	President McAleese
19–20 October 2006	Estonia	President Ilves	5–7 June 2014	France	President Hollande
3–8 May 2007	USA	President George W Bush	24–26 June 2015	Germany	President Gauck

Commonwealth tours and State Visits

DATE	COUNTRY	HOST	DATE	COUNTRY	HOST
6 February 1952	Kenya	Governor Mitchell	16 January–26 February 1961	India	President Prasad
24–25 November 1953	Bermuda	Governor Hood	1–2 March 1961	India	President Prasad
25–27 November 1953	Jamaica	Governor Foot	1–16 February 1961	Pakistan	President Ayub Khan
17–19 December 1953	Fiji	Governor Garvey	9–20 November 1961	Ghana	President Nkrumah
19–20 December 1953	Tonga	Queen Sālote Tupou III	25 November–		
23 December–30 January 1953–54	New Zealand	Governor-General Norrie	1 December 1961	Sierra Leone	Governor-General Dorman
			3–5 December 1961	Gambia	Governor Windley
3 February–1 April 1954	Australia	Governor-General Slim	30 January–1 February 1963	Canada	Governor General Vanier
5 April 1954	Cocos Islands	Governor Nicoll	2–3 February 1963	Fiji	Governor Maddocks
10–21 April 1954	Ceylon	Governor-General Ramsbotham	6–18 February 1963	New Zealand	Governor-General Fergusson
27 April 1954	Aden	Governor Hickinbotham	18 February–27 March 1963	Australia	Governor-General Sidney
28–30 April 1954	Uganda	Governor Cohen	5–13 October 1964	Canada	Governor General Vanier
3–7 May 1954	Malta	Governor Creasy	1 February 1966	Barbados	Governor Stow
10 May 1954	Gibraltar	Governor MacMillan	4–5 February 1966	British Guiana	Governor Luyt
28 January–16 February 1956	Nigeria	Governor-General Robertson	7–10 February 1966	Trinidad and Tobago	Governor-General Hochoy
12–16 October 1957	Canada	Governor General Massey	11 February 1966	Grenada	Governor Turbott
18 June–1 August 1959	Canada	Governor General Massey	13 February 1966	Saint Vincent and the Grenadines	Administrator Graham
20 January 1961	Cyprus	President Makarios III			
21 January–1 February 1961	India	President Prasad			

DATE	COUNTRY	HOST	DATE	COUNTRY	HOST
14–15 February 1966	Barbados	Governor Stow	6–8 March 1972	Malaysia	Yang di-Pertuan Agong Abdul Halim of Kedah
16 February 1966	Saint Lucia	Administrator Bryan			
18 February 1966	Dominica	Administrator Guy	19–20 March 1972	Seychelles	Governor Greatbatch
19 February 1966	Montserrat	Administrator Gibbs	24–26 March 1972	Mauritius	Governor-General Williams
20 February 1966	Antigua and Barbuda Antigua	Administrator Rose	26 March 1972	Kenya	President Kenyatta
22 February 1966	Saint Christopher-Nevis-Anguilla	Administrator Howard	25 June–5 July 1973	Canada	Governor General Michener
23 February 1966	British Virgin Islands	Administrator Staveley	31 July–4 August 1973	Canada	Governor General Michener
25 February 1966	Turks and Caicos Islands	Roger Tutt	16–17 October 1973	Fiji	Governor-General Cakobau
27–28 February 1966	Bahamas	Governor Grey	17–22 October 1973	Australia	Governor-General Hasluck
3–6 March 1966	Jamaica	Governor-General Campbell	28–29 January 1974	Cook Islands	Governor-General Blundell
			30 January–8 February 1974	New Zealand	Governor-General Blundell
29 June–5 July 1967	Canada	Governor General Michener	11 February 1974	Australia	Administrator Pickerd
14–17 November 1967	Malta	Governor-General Dorman	15–16 February 1974	New Hebrides	Resident Commissioner Houssemayne de Boulay
2–3 March 1970	Canada	Governor General Michener	18–21 February 1974	Solomon Islands	Governor Luddington
4–5 March 1970	Fiji	Governor Foster	22–27 February 1974	Papua New Guinea	High Commissioner Wilson Johnson
7 March 1970	Tonga	King Taufaʻahau Tupou IV	27–28 February 1974	Australia	Governor-General Hasluck
12–30 March 1970	New Zealand	Governor-General Porritt	16–18 February 1975	Bermuda	Governor Leather
30 March–3 May 1970	Australia	Governor-General Hasluck	18–20 February 1975	Barbados	Governor-General Scott
5–15 July 1970	Canada	Governor General Michener	20–21 February 1975	Bahamas	Governor-General Butler
			20–21 February 1975	Bermuda	Governor Leather
May 3–12 1971	Canada	Governor General Michener	26–30 April 1975	Jamaica	Governor-General Glasspole
			4–7 May 1975	Hong Kong	Governor MacLehose
18–20 February 1972	Singapore	President Sheares	13–25 July 1976	Canada	Governor General Léger
22–26, 28 February 1972	Malaysia	Yang di-Pertuan Agong Abdul Halim of Kedah	10–11 February 1977	Western Samoa	O le Ao o le Malo Malietoa Tanumafili II
29 February 1972	Brunei	Sultan Hassanal Bolkiah	14 February 1977	Tonga	King Taufaʻahau Tupou IV
29 February–2 March 1972	Malaysia	Yang di-Pertuan Agong Abdul Halim of Kedah	16–17 February 1977	Fiji	Governor-General Cakobau
5 March 1972	Singapore	President Sheares	22 February–7 March 1977	New Zealand	Governor-General Blundell
			7–23 March 1977	Australia	Governor-General Kerr
			23–26 March 1977	Papua New Guinea	Governor-General Lokoloko

DATE	COUNTRY	HOST	DATE	COUNTRY	HOST
26–30 March 1977	Australia	Governor-General Kerr	9–11 October 1985	Belize	Governor-General Gordon
14–19 October 1977	Canada	Governor-General Léger	11–18 October 1985	Bahamas	Governor-General Cash
19–20 October 1977	Bahamas	Governor-General Butler	23 October 1985	Saint Kitts and Nevis	Governor-General Arrindell
26 October 1977	British Virgin Islands	Governor Wallace	24 October 1985	Antigua and Barbuda	Governor-General Jacobs
28 October 1977	Antigua and Barbuda	Governor Jacobs	25 October 1985	Dominica	President Seignoret
31 October– 2 November 1977	Barbados	Governor-General Ward	26 October 1985	Saint Lucia	Governor-General Lewis
26 July–6 August 1978	Canada	Governor General Léger	27 October 1985	Saint Vincent and the Grenadines	Governor-General Eustace
19–22 July 1979	Tanzania	President Nyerere	28–29 October 1985	Barbados	Governor-General Springer
22–25 July 1979	Malawi	President Banda	31 October 1985	Grenada	Governor-General Scoon
25–27 July 1979	Botswana	President Seretse Khama	1–3 November 1985	Trinidad and Tobago	President Hassanali
27 July–4 August 1979	Zambia	President Kaunda			
24–28 May 1980	Australia	Governor-General Cowen	22 February–2 March 1986	New Zealand	Governor-General Reeves
26 Sep–12 October 1981	Australia	Governor-General Cowen	2–13 March 1986	Australia	Governor-General Stephen
12–20 October 1981	New Zealand	Governor-General Beattie	21–23 October 1986	Hong Kong	Governor Youde
20–21 October 1981	Australia	Governor-General Cowen	9–24 October 1987	Canada	Governor General Sauvé
21–25 October 1981	Sri Lanka	President Jayerwardene	19 April–10 May 1988	Australia	Governor-General Stephen
5–13 October 1982	Australia	Governor-General Stephen	8–11 March 1989	Barbados	Governor-General Springer
13–14 October 1982	Papua New Guinea	Governor-General Lokoloko	9–11 October 1989	Singapore	President Wee Kim Wee
18 October 1982	Solomon Islands	Governor-General Devesi	14–17 October 1989	Malaysia	Yang di-Pertuan Agong Azlan Shah
21 October 1982	Nauru	President DeRoburt	1–16 February 1990	New Zealand	Governor-General Reeves
23 October 1982	Kiribati	President Tabai	27 June–1 July 1990	Canada	Governor General Hnatyshyn
26–27 October 1982	Tuvalu	Governor-General Teo			
30 October–1 November 1982	Fiji	Governor-General Cakobau	8–10 October 1991	Namibia	President Nujoma
13 February 1983	Bermuda	Governor Posnett	10–15 October 1991	Zimbabwe	President Mugabe
13–16 February 1983	Jamaica	Governor-General Glasspole	18–25 February 1992	Australia	Governor-General Hayden
16–17 February 1983	Cayman Islands	Governor Lloyd	28–30 May 1992	Malta	President Tabone
			30 June–2 July 1992	Canada	Governor General Hnatyshyn
8–11 March 1983	Canada	Governor General Schreyer	18 February 1994	Anguilla	Governor Shave
10–14 November 1983	Kenya	President Arap Moi	19 February 1994	Dominica	President Sorhaindo
14–17 November 1983	Bangladesh	President Chowdhury	19–22 February 1994	Guyana	President Jagan
17–26 November 1983	India	President Zail Singh	22–24 February 1994	Belize	Governor-General Young
24 September–7 October 1984	Canada	Governor General Sauvé	26–27 February 1994	Cayman Islands	Governor Gore
			1–3 March 1994	Jamaica	Governor-General Cooke

DATE	COUNTRY	HOST	DATE	COUNTRY	HOST
6–8 March 1994	Bahamas	Governor-General Darling	27 February–3 March 2002	Australia	Governor-General Hollingworth
8–10 March 1994	Bermuda	Governor Waddington			
13–22 August 1994	Canada	Governor General Hnatyshyn	4–15 October 2002	Canada	Governor General Clarkson
19–25 March 1995	South Africa	President Mandela	3–6 December 2003	Nigeria	President Obasanjo
30 October– 11 November 1995	New Zealand	Governor-General Tizard	17–25 May 2005	Canada	Governor General Clarkson
23 June–2 July 1997	Canada	Governor General LeBlanc	23–26 November 2005	Malta	President Fenech Adami
6–12 October 1997	Pakistan	President Sharma	11–16 March 2006	Australia	Governor-General Jeffery
12–18 October 1997	India	President Naryanan			
17–20 September 1998	Brunei	Sultan Hassanal Bolkiah	16–18 March 2006	Singapore	President Nathan
20–23 September 1998	Malaysia	Yang di-Pertuan Agong Jaafar	20 November 2007	Malta	President Fenech Adami
			21–24 November 2007	Uganda	President Museveni
7–9 November 1999	Ghana	President Rawlings	24–26 November 2009	Bermuda	Governor Gozney
9–15 November 1999	South Africa	President Mbeki	26–28 November 2009	Trinidad and Tobago	President Richards
15 November 1999	Mozambique	President Chissano			
17 March–1 April 2000	Australia	Governor-General Deane	28 June–6 July 2010	Canada	Governor General Jean
18–20 February 2002	Jamaica	Governor-General Cooke	19–29 October 2011	Australia	Governor-General Bryce
22–27 February 2002	New Zealand	Governor-General Cartwright	26–28November 2015	Malta	President Coleiro Preca

About the publisher

St James's House is proud of its well-established reputation for producing quality publications on major royal events

ST JAMES'S HOUSE is delighted to present The Queen & Prince Philip: The Platinum Wedding Anniversary. As one of Europe's leading publishing and events companies, we have a long history of working with representatives of the Royal Family on both major national occasions and more small-scale, but no less significant, celebrations.

In 2016, we were appointed to produce the official commemorative album and souvenir programme for The Queen's 90th Birthday Celebration at Windsor Castle. We were entrusted with telling Her Majesty's story in an accessible and engaging way, and the resulting high-quality publications enabled the 25,000 attending VIPs, guests and spectators to not only enjoy the occasion to the full, but also take home an exceptional and enduring keepsake.

Four years earlier, St James's House created the official souvenir programme for the Thames Diamond Jubilee Pageant. Held in honour of Her Majesty's incredible 60 years on the throne, the pageant featured the largest flotilla of ships, boats and barges ever to be seen on the River Thames, and the programme was heralded as a huge success by the event's organisers and attendees alike.

In addition to producing quality publications for these vast landmark occasions, we also provided our expertise for a more exclusive royal gathering – the celebration of The Duke of Edinburgh's 90th birthday at

"We have a long history of working with representatives of the Royal Family on major national occasions"

Previous pages: The Queen's 90th Birthday Celebration at Windsor Castle, 2016

Opposite: The accompanying commemorative album, as produced by St James's House

Windsor Castle. Coordinated by St James's House, the Rolls-Royce Enthusiasts' Club and the Prince Philip Trust Fund, the event was attended and thoroughly enjoyed by Prince Philip, who was treated to a cavalcade of luxury veteran motorcars before being honoured at a private reception in the Great Hall.

Forthcoming projects for St James's House include a commemorative album to accompany the Royal Air Force's centenary celebrations, which will include a parade and flypast on The Mall.

In the meantime, however, it simply falls on us to wish Her Majesty The Queen and The Duke of Edinburgh the very warmest of congratulations on achieving 70 years of marriage – happy platinum wedding anniversary your Majesty and your Royal Highness.

www.stjamess.org

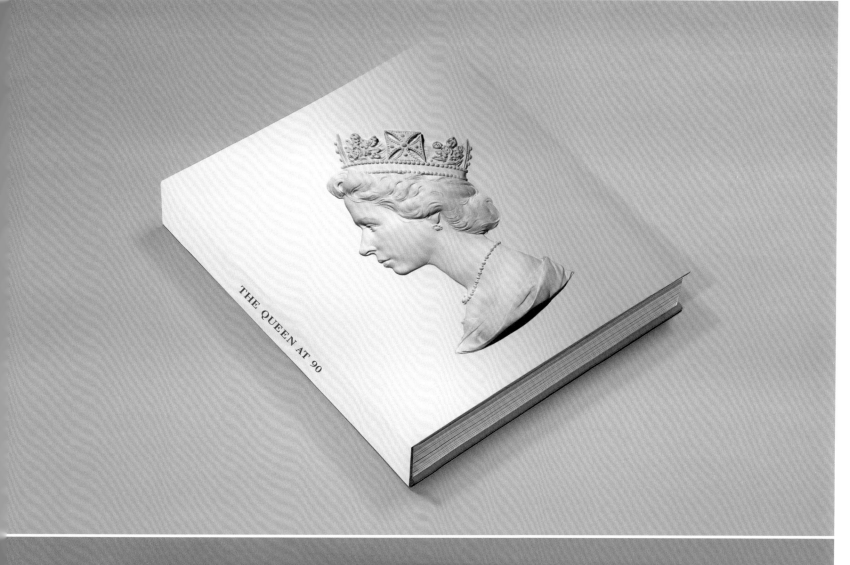

THE QUEEN AT 90

"I am looking forward
to a busy 2016, though
I have been warned I may
have Happy Birthday
sung to me more than
once or twice"

Her Majesty The Queen,
Christmas Message, Christmas Day 2015

Credits

St James's House
298 Regents Park Road
London N3 2SZ

T: 020 8371 4000
E: publishing@stjamess.org
W: www.stjamess.org

Chief Executive
Richard Freed
richard.freed@stjamess.org

Managing Director
Stephen van der Merwe
stephen.vdm@stjamess.org

Sales Director
Richard Golbourne
r.golbourne@stjamess.org

Communications Director
Ben Duffy
ben.duffy@stjamess.org

Head of Editorial
Stephen Mitchell
stephen.mitchell@stjamess.org

Deputy Editor
John Lewis

Chief Writer
Robert Jobson

Head of Creative
Anna Danby
anna.danby@stjamess.org

Designers
Aniela Gil
Natalie Clay

Cover photograph
Everett Collection Inc / Alamy Stock Photo

Photography
Getty Images